I0460192

Appointed Pen Publishing
ISBN 979-8-89778-463-9
STATEN HOUSE

Cover design by: Art Painter
Library of Congress Control Number: 2018675309
Printed in the United States of America

To every Yah-fearing daughter, wife, mother, and sister who has chosen to rise,
To the women who are no longer conforming, but transforming
—
This is for you....

For the ones who are ready to unlearn the lies, walk in truth,
And reclaim our set-apart roles with grace, wisdom, and strength.
May you be reminded that you were born for such a time as this.
Let this be your charge, your confirmation, and your call to purpose.

With love and reverence—
Your sis ChayilYah

To all the Yah fearing Elders, Fathers, Husbands, Brothers, Sons....

I didn't know I needed you.
The enemy ran in and destroyed our homes and the locust ate
because no one stood at the gate
The man became burden and by the oppressors they were beat
because the woman refused to be a help meet
we walked into many rooms and was devoured by the dragon
serpent
because the woman had no discernment
we've created broken homes and made our idols a statute
because we lacked character and virtue
we were told within is the kingdom
yet we never cultivated maturity where is the wisdom?
theres no love but hate and jealousy
little do we know this is being passed down as legacy
a generation of fear, lack of faith and weak endurance
because there are no leaders to give reassurance
they scream we don't need you
we scream we can be independent apart from you
only because we didn't know our role
all because we believed we weren't apart of the goal

INTRODUCTION

Throughout history, women have been entrusted with the sacred duty of safeguarding their homes and communities. In the biblical context, this role extends beyond physical protection to encompass spiritual guardianship. A biblical woman is not merely a nurturer; she is also a watchwoman, a discerner of spirits, and a keeper of the gates. Her influence is woven into the fabric of her household, shaping its spiritual climate and determining what enters and what is cast out.

This book explores the profound role of the biblical woman as a spiritual gatekeeper. It examines her divine calling to stand guard over her home and family, ensuring that only righteousness, wisdom, and holiness take root. The Scriptures provide a wealth of wisdom on this subject, revealing that the role of a gatekeeper is not a passive one but an active, strategic, and divinely appointed position. From the prophetess Deborah, who led Israel with courage and discernment, to Miriam, who stood as a pillar of guidance and praise among her people, the Bible offers powerful examples of women who embraced their roles as spiritual sentinels.

Central to this role is the concept of the "gates." In the ancient world, city gates were places of authority, judgment, and decision-making. They determined what entered and what remained outside. In the same way, a woman's home has spiritual gates—portals through which influences, ideas, and energies flow. The responsibility of a biblical woman is to recognize these gates, discern their impact, and ensure that her home remains a sanctuary of holiness and peace.

This book lays the foundation for understanding the biblical and spiritual basis of a woman's role and the "Art of Becoming" all that YHWH has designed her to be. It will delve into the significance of discernment, prayer, and righteous authority in maintaining the sanctity of the home and community. By exploring biblical principles, real-life applications, and the timeless wisdom of the Most High, this book will empower women to embrace their divine assignment with confidence, wisdom, and unwavering faith.

As you journey through these pages, remember a righteous woman is not born; she is shaped, refined, and strengthened through her walk with Her Heavenly Father. She becomes. This book is a guide to the 12 gates of transformation—an intentional process of stepping into the fullness of who Yah has called you to be. Each gate is an area of mastery, a path to wholeness (*Tamim*), and a key to unlocking your divine purpose. To walk through these gates is to embrace spiritual growth, wisdom, and power. It is to become a woman of Yah who is unwavering, discerning, and built for endurance.

A gatekeeper stands at the threshold between the holy and the profane, the seen and the unseen. She protects what is sacred—her mind, her spirit, her home, and her community. She is not easily swayed by the distractions of the world because she moves with purpose, clothed in wisdom and virtue. This book will guide you through each of these gates, preparing you to walk in spiritual maturity and embody the principles that make a woman **"Tamim"**—whole, complete, and aligned with Yah's will.

The 12 Gates of Becoming Tamim

1. **The Art of Being a Spiritual Gatekeeper** – "She don't play 'bout herself."
   A woman of Yah sets clear *boundaries*—physically, emotionally, and spiritually. She *guards* her peace and does not allow disrespect. To become whole, you must first *protect* what Yah has given you.

2. **The Art of Fear** – "She knows Who she answers to."
   The fear of Yah is the beginning of wisdom. She moves with *respect* and *accountability*, knowing that her steps are ordered and that she answers to a higher authority.

3. **The Art of Being an Ally (*Ezer*)** – "She's, his rib."
   A righteous woman is a divine partner, a **helper** fit for her husband, and a *support system* that strengthens the family structure. She understands the power of her role as an *ezer*—a *strong ally*, not a subordinate.

4. **The Art of Discernment and Prudence** – "She peep game and read the room."
   She is not easily deceived. She is *observant, spiritually in tune,* and *understands unspoken dynamics* before acting or speaking. *Prudence* keeps her steps steady.

5. **The Art of Virtue** – "She walking right."
   Integrity and righteousness are her foundation. She moves in a way that commands respect and reflects her spiritual values. She is clothed in virtue, which is evident in how she *speaks, acts,* and *carries herself*.

6. **The Art of Wisdom** – "She got old soul knowledge."
   A woman of Yah doesn't just accumulate information; she *applies wisdom*. She carries the weight of *generational understanding* and *timeless truths*, using them to build and sustain her household and community.

7. **The Art of Servanthood** – "She the backbone."
   She understands that servanthood is not weakness—it is strength. She holds everything together through her *service, love,* and *humility*, supporting those around her with grace.

8. **The Art of Inner Beauty** – "She shine from the inside out."
   True beauty comes from within. Her *faith, character,* and *kindness* radiate outward, setting her apart from those who focus only on external appearances.

9. **The Art of Endurance** – "She built for this."
   Life brings trials, but a woman of Yah endures. She is *resilient, steadfast,* and *unwavering*, knowing that perseverance refines her faith and strengthens her spirit.

10. **The Art of Legacy** – "She leaving her mark."
    She is not just living for today—she is building for generations to come. Her *actions, teachings, and values* create a legacy that will impact her children and her community long after she is gone.

11. **The Art of Manifestation** – "She spoke it, now she walks in it."
    Faith without works is dead. She does not just dream—*she moves*. She co-creates greatness with Yah, bringing her vision to life through faith and action.

12. **The Art of Becoming Perfect (*Tamim*)** – "She handles hers."
    Perfection in the Hebraic sense is about wholeness, not flawlessness. A woman of Yah is dependable, responsible, and spiritually mature. She *continuously grows, refines, and aligns* herself with Yah's purpose.

Each gate represents a transformative step, a refining process that brings you closer to *spiritual maturity*. This book is not just about *theory*—it is about *application*. It will challenge you to *reflect, adjust, and elevate*. To become "Tamim" is to embrace the fullness of what it means to be a woman of Yah. It is a *lifelong process* of *growth, discipline, and faith*.

So, are you ready to walk through the gates? Are you ready to step into your *purpose, refine* your spirit, and *embody* the wisdom and strength of the righteous women before you? The journey begins *now*.

Let's walk.

Testimonial By: Chayilyah Segulah

When you're single, there are so many things we cry out to the Creator for—especially in our loneliness, our fears, and sometimes, in our ignorance. I remember being in that exact place. I was overwhelmed, tired of carrying everything on my own, desiring protection, longing for love, craving companionship, and dreaming of having children. So, I did what many of us do—I wrote out a list of everything I wanted in a husband: physical qualities, emotional depth, spiritual integrity and I prayed over that list every single day with faith and expectancy.

But what I didn't know at the time was this: I wasn't just praying for a man. I was actually praying for a process—a refining journey that would begin with me.

The Most High used that very list to show me everything I needed to become. What I thought was a prayer for a husband turned into a divine invitation for transformation. It took four years from that initial prayer before I was found by my husband. Four years that became the foundation for everything I would carry into wifehood, motherhood, and into becoming a woman of purpose. Those four years didn't delay me—they built me.

This book is the story of that transformation. It's how Yah prepared me for the very prayer I thought I was ready for. It's how He matured the desire of my heart and turned it into a ministry, a legacy, and a powerful testimony of His timing and sovereignty. Yah took my "want"—rooted in survival and loneliness—and redefined it with purpose, vision, and generational breakthrough.

Through this journey, I discovered that I was already equipped with everything I would need to support, nurture, and grow alongside my husband and children. But first, I had to step into my role. Not just the title of "wife"—but the function, the posture, the spiritual responsibility of becoming the living details to the vision Yah assigned

1

to our home.

Knowing my role gave me peace. It eliminated unnecessary stress and confusion. It helped me discern when to intercede, when to give space, and when to trust The Most High's work in my husband's life. It deepened my respect and honor for him and allowed me to love him more fiercely because I saw how The Most High was molding him—just as He was molding me.

This perspective changed everything: how I prayed, how I responded, how I honored my covenant. I learned to stop trying to "fix" my husband and instead give my concerns to Abba. To my amazement, I would watch my husband respond to the very things I prayed in secret. It increased my faith, refocused my heart, and reminded me that The Creator is deeply involved in the most intricate parts of our lives—if we're willing to surrender everything to Him.

The depth of your surrender determines the depth of His involvement. *Marriage, purpose, finances, family—it all hinges on how much control you're willing to release.*

This book is not a formula—it's a testimony. A real, raw, and redemptive look at how The Most High answers prayers not just by giving us what we want, but by preparing us to become who we're called to be.

So, wherever you are on your journey—single, waiting, preparing, happily married or newly married—take heart. Nothing happens overnight, but every moment is shaping something sacred. Let Elohim guide every step. Let Him into every part of who you are. And watch how He reveals who you were always meant to become. Enjoy pieces of my testimony at the begin of each chapter.

Becoming A Guard Over My Gates

My very first lesson as a single woman was learning how to silence the noise—externally and internally. The only way I could truly do that was by sitting in intentional, extended blocks of silence. That silence became my training ground.

To be a guard—a spiritual gatekeeper—meant I had to become more aware. It wasn't just about knowing how to say no; it was about discerning what needed to be allowed in and what needed to be cast out. I began to train my awareness through meditation and deep study of Scripture. I needed to understand: What is The Most High saying? How does His voice sound? What does His judgment look like? If I was going to walk in spiritual authority, I had to first know His voice intimately.

That led me to ask deeper questions: What are the parameters of this choice I'm making to become a spiritual guard? What am I truly willing to give up? What are my morals—and what are Abba's?

Everything began to shift.

*I changed the music I listened to and only played worship throughout my day. I replaced TV with spiritual books, and to my surprise, I didn't miss television at all. My appetite—spiritually and physically—began to change. As I diligently searched the Scriptures, I realized that the Hebrew word **"Shanan"** means "to sharpen" or "to wet"—and that's exactly what was happening to me. The more I immersed myself in Yah's Word, the sharper my discernment became, and my taste—both naturally and spiritually—began to align with His will.*

Some days, I barely ate, not out of restriction, but because I was so full of the Word and so focused on the transformation happening inside of me. My words, my temperament, and even my reactions began to change. I was being refined.

I came to understand that becoming a spiritual gatekeeper started with one thing: guarding my own gates. What I allowed into my eyes, ears, mind, and spirit had power. And the more I guarded those gates, the stronger, more disciplined, and more spiritually aligned I became.

To be continued...

CHAPTER 1 THE ART OF BEING A SPIRITUAL GATEKEEPER

"She doesn't play 'bout herself."

A woman who understands her role as a spiritual gatekeeper moves with wisdom, vigilance, and authority. She is the guardian of her home, watchwoman of her community, and the intercessor who stands in the gap. To be a gatekeeper is to be entrusted with access—to what enters, what remains, and what is cast out. It is a high calling, a divine responsibility, and a role that shapes the spiritual atmosphere of a household and beyond.

In ancient times, the position of a gatekeeper was one of immense responsibilities. The city gates were not only physical structures but places of judgment, decision-making, and governance. Spiritually, a woman is assigned this same role over her home and family, standing watch over the influences that attempt to enter.

Proverbs 14:1 state, *"Every wise woman builds her house, but the foolish one tears it down with her own hands."* A wise woman guards her household diligently, ensuring that what is built stands firm in righteousness. She does not permit disorder, deception, or unrighteousness to take root, for she understands that her home is a sacred space.

The Scripture often speaks of gates as places of power, authority, and transition. Gates symbolize control over what is permitted to enter and what is expelled. The spiritual gatekeeper must be aware of the many doors through which influences enter her home-physically, emotionally, and spiritually. These gates include:

1. *The Eye/Eyes (- עינים Eynayim) Gate – What is seen within the home, from entertainment to the actions of those present. The eyes are the gateway to the soul. In Hebraic thought, what one sees affects their inner being.* **Psalm 101:3** *– "I will set no wicked thing before my eyes: I hate the work of them that turn aside; it shall not cleave to me."*

   - What one looks at influences their spirit and morality. **Numbers 15:39** *– "And you shall have the tassel, that you may look upon it and remember all the commandments of YHWH and do them, and that you may not follow after your own heart and your own eyes, after which you used to go astray."* **(The tzitzit (fringes) were given as a visual reminder to keep the commandments and not be led astray by sight.)**
   - Focus should be maintained on righteousness and not on distractions leading to sin. **Proverbs 4:25-27** *– "Let your eyes look straight ahead, and your eyelids look right before you."*

Cultural Understanding: The eye is linked to ayin hara (the evil eye), which represents envy and negative perception. Protecting the eyes from unclean things and maintaining a pure gaze is crucial. In Hebrew thought, to "lift one's eyes" (נשא עיניו) Can mean to direct attention, desire, or hope toward something, whether good or evil.

2. **The Ears (- אוזניים Oznayim) Gate** – What is spoken and heard. Words carry power, and a woman must be diligent in filtering out destructive speech.

- **Proverbs 18:21** teaches, *"Death and life are in the power of the tongue."* Hearing is a key concept in Hebraic culture. To "hear" (shema) is not merely to perceive sound but to obey.
- **Deuteronomy 6:4** – *"Shema, Yisrael: YHWH Eloheinu, YHWH Echad."* The Shema prayer emphasizes listening as an act of devotion and obedience.
- **Proverbs 2:2** – *"Make your ear attentive to wisdom and incline your heart to understanding."* Listening is the first step in acquiring wisdom.
- **Isaiah 30:21** – *"And your ears shall hear a word behind you, saying, 'This is the way, walk in it,' when you turn to the right or when you turn to the left."* The spiritually attuned ear can discern divine direction.

Cultural Understanding: The Hebrew word **"Shema"** (hear) means more than just hearing; it implies obedience. In Biblical culture, hearing and acting were one and the same. Closing one's ears to wisdom was equated with rebellion, while listening with understanding led to righteousness.

3. **The Heart (- לב Lev) Gate** – What is allowed to take root in the center for your emotions and spirit. Are love, peace, and joy being cultivated, or is bitterness, resentment, and anxiety taking hold?

- **Proverbs 4:23** warns, *"Keep thy heart with all diligence, for out of it are the issues of life."* The heart in Hebrew thought is not just emotions but also thoughts, will, and decisions. The heart directs a person's entire life.

- *Jeremiah 17:9-10* – *"The heart is deceitful above all things, and desperately wicked; who can know it? I, YHWH, search the heart, I test the mind, to give every man according to his ways."* The heart must be aligned with YHWH, as it can be deceptive if left unchecked.
- *Ezekiel 36:26* – *"And I will give you a new heart, and a new spirit I will put within you. And I will remove the heart of stone from your flesh and give you a heart of flesh."* YHWH promises spiritual transformation through a purified heart.

Cultural Understanding: In Hebrew thought, the **"Leb"** (heart) was the seat of intellect and will, not just emotions. A righteous heart was considered necessary for covenant faithfulness. The phrase *"circumcise your heart" (Deuteronomy 10:16)* refers to removing stubbornness and becoming fully devoted to YHWH.

4. *The Mind (- מוח Moach) Gate* – *What is meditated upon daily. Thoughts shape actions, and a woman must ensure her mind is renewed in the Word of YHWH.*

- *Romans 12:2* instructs, *"Be not conformed to this world, but be ye transformed by the renewing of your mind."* The mind is the center of thought, meditation, and understanding. In Hebraic thought, guarding the mind is essential for wisdom, righteousness, and faithfulness.
- *Isaiah 26:3* – *"You will keep him in perfect peace, whose mind is stayed on You, because he trusts in You."* The mind should be steadfast in trusting YHWH,

leading to peace and stability.

- **Proverbs 3:5-6** – *"Trust in YHWH with all your heart, and do not lean on your own understanding. In all your ways acknowledge Him, and He will make your paths straight."* The mind should not rely on personal intellect alone but be submitted to divine wisdom.
- **Deuteronomy 6:5** – *"And you shall love YHWH your Elohim with all your heart, with all your soul, and with all your strength."* Hebraically, *"heart" (lev)* includes the mind, meaning one must love YHWH with full intellect and will.

Cultural Understanding: In Hebraic culture, the *"Moach"* (mind) is not viewed separately from the heart but as interconnected. The Hebrews did not compartmentalize emotions and intellect; instead, wisdom was seen as both spiritual and intellectual. Renewing the mind through Torah study was a daily practice to ensure alignment with YHWH's will.

5. **Mouth (- פה Peh) Gate**–The words you speak daily is very important. The mouth is a powerful gate, responsible for speaking blessings or curses.

   - **Proverbs 18:21** – *"Death and life are in the power of the tongue, and those who love it will eat its fruit."* Words have power to create or destroy.
   - **Psalm 141:3** – *"Set a guard, O YHWH, over my mouth; keep watch over the door of my lips."* A wise person guards their speech to prevent sin.
   - **Proverbs 15:4** – *"A wholesome tongue is a tree of life, but perverseness in it breaks the spirit."* Speech should be life-giving, not destructive.

Cultural Understanding: Words were seen as binding and powerful; vows and oaths were taken seriously. In Torah culture, blessings (ברכות) And curses (קללות) Had spiritual weight. Speaking in alignment with Torah was a mark of righteousness.

The *mind, eyes, ears, mouth, and heart* are all spiritual gates that must be guarded. In this culture, righteousness comes from aligning these gates with Torah principles:

- **Mind** → Keep it focused on wisdom and YHWH's instruction.
- **Eyes** → Avoid distractions and sin, keeping vision clear.
- **Ears** → Listen to truth and obey.
- **Mouth** → Speak life, avoid wicked speech.
- **Heart** → Keep it pure, as it directs all actions.

By **watching over these gates**, woman can ensure spiritual integrity and alignment with YHWH's will for her household. The role of a biblical woman as a spiritual gatekeeper is one of profound significance. A custodian entrusted with the spiritual well-being of her loved ones rooted in the fear of Yahuah and guided by the principles of wisdom. Gates are more than just barriers, entryways or a way to control flow entry/exit. In the Bible, the people of The Most High understood the significance of gates very well. Think about the gates around you, what are they made of? What significance do they hold? Do they bring comfort, aesthetics, safety, or separation? In addition, some gates may have gatekeepers or security guards to provide reinforcement or keen vigilance.

To be a spiritual gatekeeper is to complete the task Chawah started which was to gain hold of the vision and promises given to her by Adam for her your house and community. She was supposed to acknowledge the sovereignty of Yah and recognize him as the foundation upon which life and all faith are built. We are called to cultivate an environment where prayer becomes the heartbeat of daily life. Where praise is on the tongues of all who enter in. Our role is one of strength because our praise has become our garment or character. Surely in a place filled with praise, there's no room for the serpent to roam freely. we should diligently comb over what enters and leaves the house. While poking holes into everyone who knocks at the door, even the ones who live there because they're dusting off the cares of the world at the entryway.

A spiritual gatekeeper must be anchored in prayer. Hannah, the mother of Samuel, exemplifies this in **1 Samuel 1:9-20.** When she desired a child, she did not accept barrenness as her portion—she interceded at the temple, pouring out her soul before The Most High. Her persistence in prayer changed the course of her family's legacy and birthed a prophet who would anoint kings.

A woman who prays is a woman who governs. She does not react to circumstances in fear but instead seeks the wisdom of The Creator, knowing that spiritual battles are won in the secret place before they manifest in the natural. She intercedes for her husband, covering him in wisdom and strength. She prays for her children, shaping their destinies before they step into them. She prays for her home, ensuring that it is a place of refuge and righteousness.

To be a spiritual gatekeeper is not to live in fear of the enemy's schemes; it is to walk in the authority given by YHWH. The **Proverbs 31** woman is described as one who watches over the affairs of her household and does not eat the bread of idleness **(Proverbs 31:27).** She is proactive, not passive. She understands that her presence alone has the power to shift the atmosphere. Walking in this authority means:

- **Declaring the Word over your home and family daily.**
- **Removing anything that does not align with holiness and peace.**
- **Teaching your children and household the ways of righteousness.**
- **Living as an example of faith, wisdom, and obedience.**

Every woman is called to be a gatekeeper in some capacity. Whether she is married or single, a mother or a mentor, her presence influences the spiritual climate of her surroundings.

To step into this role:

1. **Seek Wisdom in the Word** – Study the examples of righteous women who stood guard over their homes and communities.
2. **Establish a Prayer Routine** – Dedicate time to covering your household, even before challenges arise.
3. **Be Discerning** – Ask YHWH for insight into what is affecting your family and how to handle it.
4. **Set the Standard** – Do not compromise on the values that align with holiness. Lead with love and conviction.

Biblical Examples of Spiritual Gatekeepers

- **Deborah:** A prophetess, judge, and warrior, Deborah led Israel with wisdom and courage **(Judges 4-5)**. She was a gatekeeper in the truest sense, ensuring the people turned their hearts back to YHWH and leading them to victory against their oppressors.

- **Miriam:** As the sister of Moses, Miriam played a key role in safeguarding and guiding the Israelite people **(Exodus 15:20-21)**. She led in worship and was instrumental in maintaining the spiritual morale of the people.

- **Abigail:** The wife of Nabal, Abigail acted as a gatekeeper of peace and wisdom when she interceded to prevent David from taking vengeance **(1 Samuel 25:23-33)**. Through her discernment, she safeguarded her household from destruction.

Being a spiritual gatekeeper is both a privilege and a responsibility. It is the art of watching, praying, discerning, and protecting. It is the art of becoming a woman who not only builds her home but secures it in righteousness. As you grow in this role, may you stand firm in faith, wisdom, and the knowledge that you have been divinely positioned to guard what is precious in the sight of YHWH.

To gain a deeper understanding of what it means to be a spiritual gatekeeper from a Hebraic perspective, we must examine the profound symbolism and cultural context found in Hebrew scripture and tradition. This role carries both spiritual and practical significance, reflecting the ancient wisdom surrounding community and family responsibilities.

1. **Guardians of the Covenant**: In the Hebrew Bible, gatekeepers were entrusted with safeguarding the entrances to cities, temples, and homes. This role symbolized not only physical protection but also spiritual vigilance. As spiritual gatekeepers, women are called to uphold the covenant relationship with TMH—a covenant that encompasses faithfulness, obedience, and reverence for His commandments. This duty reflects the broader Hebrew understanding of the family as a microcosm of the covenant community.

2. Gateways to Blessing: Gates in ancient Hebrew culture were seen as places of blessing and judgment. Gatekeepers controlled access to these pivotal thresholds. Similarly, women as spiritual gatekeepers have the profound privilege of opening doors to spiritual blessings within their families and communities. Through prayer, Torah study, and acts of kindness, they channel divine blessings into the lives of those under their care.

3. Transmitters of Tradition: Hebraic tradition places a strong emphasis on the transmission of faith from one generation to the next. Women played a vital role in this process, imparting knowledge of Torah and Jewish practices within the home. As spiritual gatekeepers, women preserve and perpetuate the spiritual heritage of their ancestors, ensuring continuity in the covenantal relationship with God.

4. Role in Family and Community Life: Women in ancient Israel were often the primary caretakers of the household, responsible for nurturing the spiritual well-being of their families. This encompassed not only the practical aspects of daily life but also the cultivation of faith, prayer, and moral values. The Hebrew concept of *"eshet chayil"* (a woman of valor) celebrates women who embody strength, wisdom, and righteousness in their roles as spiritual gatekeepers.

5. Intercessors and Mediators: In Hebraic thought, women are seen as powerful intercessors and mediators between heaven and earth. The matriarchs of Israel—Sarah, Rebecca, Rachel, and Leah—exemplify this role through their prayers and acts of righteousness.

As spiritual gatekeepers, women are called to stand in the gap, advocating for their families before God and seeking His guidance and protection. By embracing the role of spiritual gatekeeper from a Hebraic perspective, women not only fulfill a sacred duty but also participate in a timeless tradition that honors the sanctity of family, community, and covenant relationship with God. This perspective underscores the vital importance of women as pillars of faith and guardians of spiritual heritage within the tapestry of Hebrew life and tradition.

some real-life, culturally relevant examples of how this plays out in everyday Hebraic life:

1. She Guards Her Home Like a Fortress

It's Erev Shabbat, and she's cleaning her home, sweeping out both the dust and the spiritual clutter. She lights her candles, prays over her household, and anoints her doorposts with oil. She won't let just anybody walk through her doors—energy matters. Before letting guests in, she discerns their spirit. If their vibe is off, she prays for wisdom. *"A wise woman builds her house, but a foolish one tears it down with her hands."* **(Proverbs 14:1)**

She doesn't play 'bout herself—or her house.

2. She's Careful About What She Listens To

Her girls send her a video of the latest gossip in the community— some drama about who did what on social media. She shakes her head and deletes it. She doesn't have time for that. Instead, she turns on Torah teachings or Hebrew praise music while she cooks. She protects her ears because she knows that what she hears feeds her spirit. *"Keep your heart with all diligence, for out of it are the issues of life."* **(Proverbs 4:23)**

She doesn't play 'bout herself—or her peace.

3. She Doesn't Let Just Any Man Have Access to Her

She's at the market picking up lamb and bitter herbs for Pesach when a smooth-talking brother tries to get her attention. "Shalom, sis, you looking righteous today." She smiles but keeps it moving. She doesn't entertain random conversations, especially with men who aren't walking in Torah. She carries herself with dignity because she knows her worth. *"Give not your strength unto women, nor your ways to that which destroyeth kings."* **(Proverbs 31:3)**

She doesn't play 'bout herself—or her virtue.

4. She Protects Her Spirit from Evil Influences

At a family gathering, everyone is talking about manifesting wealth and burning sage to cleanse bad energy. They tell her she's being "extra" when she says she doesn't participate in New Age practices. She doesn't argue, but she stands firm. She trusts in YAH, not foreign spiritual customs. *"Learn not the way of the heathen."* **(Jeremiah 10:2)**

She doesn't play 'bout herself—or her faith.

5. She Knows Who Her Sisters Are

She has a tight circle of righteous women—sisters who fast with her, pray with her, and hold her accountable. When she's feeling weak, they remind her who she is. When they see her slipping, they correct her in love. She doesn't surround herself with women who thrive on mess, jealousy, or negativity. *"Iron sharpens iron; so a man sharpens the countenance of his friend."* **(Proverbs 27:17)**

She doesn't play 'bout herself—or her sisterhood.

6. She Walks in Modesty and Strength

It's a hot day in Texas, but she still wraps her head and covers her body with grace. People ask why she doesn't dress like other women, why she doesn't show a little more skin. She tells them, "I don't dress for attention; I dress for YAH." She understands that her body is a temple, and she carries herself like a daughter of the King. *"Strength and honor are her clothing, and she shall rejoice in time to come."* **(Proverbs 31:25)**

She doesn't play 'bout herself—or her dignity.

Selah moment:

As a spiritual gate keeper where are your boundaries for your family? Do you have any boundaries? Are you just allowing the enemy within to create a house of emotionalism? Or are you becoming a new type of spiritual gatekeeper with the word NO on your lips! Remember the virtuous woman rose early not for just for the people she poured into daily but, to meet daily with the giver of her strength. The more you do daily should equal the amount of time you give to TMH. You can't guard what you don't know!

The Gatekeeper's Watch

I stand at the door with a heart full of prayer,
A sentinel placed by His mercy and care.
Not with sword, nor with shield made of steel,
But with faith, with love, with a spirit that kneels.

The winds of the world may howl at our gate,
Temptation and trial may whisper of fate.
Yet I press my ear to the voice of the King,
And stand as a wall, as the Malakim sing.

I guard the threshold where peace must reside,
Where wisdom and virtue forever abide.
No darkness may enter, no falsehood take hold,
For this home is a garden, its fruit pure as gold.

I cover my husband in prayer's gentle light,
Lifting his hands when he wearies from fight.
A watchman, a keeper, a beacon so bright,
Rooted in truth, clothed in His might.

My words are a river that nourish the land,
Soft as the rain, yet strong as the sand.
I speak life, I speak grace, I speak heaven's decree,
For a wife's sacred calling is to intercede.

O daughters of Zion, rise to your post!
Stand firm in His wisdom, be led by the Host!
For a gatekeeper's watch is not just for show,
It's the heart of the home where righteousness flows.

So, I stand at the door with a heart full of prayer,
A vessel, a servant, His will to declare.
No thief shall pass, no storm shall undo,
For this house is His temple—
And I am its truth.

The Fear That Transformed Me

Whew—this was one of the hardest parts of being single: developing the fear of Yah. Not the kind that pushes you away, but the kind that pulls you in deeper, humbles you, and exposes the parts of yourself you didn't even know were standing in the way.

As I grew stronger in my role as a spiritual gatekeeper—a true "boundary princess," if you will—the more I learned about Yah, the more I fell in love with Him. But at the same time, that love awakened a deep, holy fear. Not fear of punishment, but a reverence so raw and real that I began to see myself for who I truly was: filthy rags. Unworthy to stand before such a righteous and holy Elohim.

The more I learned, the more vulnerable I felt. I realized I wasn't truly doing what He required—I was moving based on what I thought He wanted, not what He commanded. And how could I even claim to be obedient if I didn't know the rules? That realization shook me. The thinness of my spiritual foundation frightened me—but that fear drove me to build. To grow. To tighten up.

I began to understand the weight of my worship. The sacredness of reverence. The power of obedience. I came face-to-face with the Shema—Deuteronomy 6:4-6—and for the first time, I really saw it: to love Yah with all your heart, soul, and might is a call to abandon everything you think you are and fully surrender to who He created you to be.

It was a breaking, but a holy one. I had to let go of my ideas, my plans, and even my identity as I knew it. I had no say in the vessel He formed in my mother's womb. I was made for His glory, not my own.

Then Psalm 78 echoed in my spirit: We are but wind. That verse fortified my trust and stripped me of the illusion of control. I realized I had encountered the One True Sovereign—the Master over every detail of my life. And even in that clarity, I knew I was only at the beginning.

So many questions still lingered in my heart, but now they were coming from a place of awe, not anxiety.

To be continued...

CHAPTER 2 THE ART OF FEAR

"She knows Who she answers to."

A woman who walks in the fear of Yahuah moves with purpose, reverence, and accountability. This fear is not the kind that paralyzes—it is not terror or dread—it is a deep, abiding respect and awe for the Most High. It shapes the way she speaks, the way she acts, and the way she carries herself in the world. She is not reckless, for she understands that every step she takes is observed by Yahuah. She does not move aimlessly, for she knows she is part of something greater than herself.

What is the Fear of Yahuah?

In Hebrew, the word for fear used in Scripture is *"Yirah"* (יִרְאָה,) which means reverence, awe, and deep respect. It is the kind of fear that causes a person to bow their head in humility before the greatness of Yahuah. **Proverbs 1:7** tells us, *"The fear of Yahuah is the beginning of knowledge: but fools despise wisdom and instruction."* This kind of fear is foundational—it is the starting point of wisdom, the lens through which we see the world rightly.

In the ancient Hebraic world, the fear of Yahuah was the mark of a righteous woman. She was the cornerstone of the home, the silent yet steady force that shaped the spiritual climate of her family. Women like Sarah, who honored her husband but ultimately placed her trust in Yahuah's promises **(Genesis 18:12-15)**, and the midwives Shiphrah and Puah, who feared Yahuah more than Pharaoh and saved the lives of Hebrew babies **(Exodus 1:15-21)**, demonstrated this holy reverence.

To fear Yahuah is to acknowledge His sovereignty in all things. It means submitting to His commandments, not out of obligation alone, but out of love and trust in His divine order. A woman who fears Yahuah walks differently—her steps are measured, her words are seasoned with wisdom, and her presence carries the weight of someone who knows who she is and whose she is.

Reverence for Yahuah is the foundation of a biblical woman's life. It is not merely a posture of obedience but a deep, abiding awe for the Most High, shaping her thoughts, actions, and decisions. In the biblical context, the word "fear" of Yahuah does not imply terror but rather an overwhelming respect and honor for His holiness, sovereignty, and divine authority.

The Proverbs 31 woman is perhaps the most well-known example. *Proverbs 31:30* declares, *"Favor is deceitful, and beauty is vain: but a woman that fears Yahuah, she shall be praised."* This verse is often quoted, but its depth is sometimes overlooked. A woman's greatest honor was not her outward appearance or charm but her deep-rooted fear of Yahuah. It was this fear that guided her decisions, shaped her character, and made her worthy of praise.

A woman who truly fears Yahuah:

- **Moves with Intention** – She does not act carelessly because she knows her life is a testimony.
- **Speaks with Wisdom** – Her words are measured, reflecting the teachings of Torah **(Proverbs 31:26)**.

- **Guards Her Home** – She protects the spiritual atmosphere of her household, ensuring that only righteousness dwells within **(Proverbs 14:1).**

- **Holds Herself Accountable** – She does not justify wrongdoing but seeks correction and growth **(Psalm 139:23-24)**.

- **Leads By Example** – Her fear of Yahuah influences those around her, calling them to a higher standard of living.

Understanding the Fear of Yahuah

The Scriptures declare, *"The fear of Yahuah is the beginning of wisdom, and the knowledge of the Holy One is understanding"* (Proverbs 9:10). This principle establishes that true wisdom does not originate from human intellect but from a heart fully submitted to the Most High. A biblical woman who walks in reverence for Yahuah operates in divine wisdom, discernment, and spiritual maturity.

This fear is not about shrinking away but about drawing near with humility, recognizing Yahuah's authority over all aspects of life. *Ecclesiastes 12:13* reinforces this: *"Let us hear the conclusion of the whole matter: Fear Yahuah, and keep His commandments: for this is the whole duty of man."* For a woman devoted to righteousness, this principle is the guiding force behind her decisions and conduct.

A woman who fears Yahuah does not operate in self-reliance but places her trust fully in Him. Her reverence influences:

1. **Her Speech:** She speaks with wisdom and grace, knowing that her words carry weight. *Proverbs 31:26* states, *"She openeth her mouth with wisdom; and in her tongue is the law of kindness."*

2. **Her Decisions:** She seeks the will of Yahuah in all things, acknowledging Him in her ways **(Proverbs 3:5-6)**.

3. **Her Relationships:** She carries herself with dignity and

honor, aligning her interactions with righteousness.

4. **Her Leadership in the Home and Community:** She leads through example, demonstrating faith and integrity.

5. **Her Resilience in Trials:** She remains steadfast in faith, understanding that challenges refine her character **(James 1:2-4)**.

Biblical Examples of Women Who Feared Yahuah

- **Sarah (Genesis 18:12, 1 Peter 3:5-6):** She honored Yahuah and walked in submission to His promises, demonstrating faith even in uncertainty.

- **Hannah (1 Samuel 1:10-20):** Her deep reverence for Yahuah led her to persistent prayer and unwavering trust, resulting in the birth of the prophet Samuel.

- **Esther (Esther 4:16):** She exhibited boldness and faith in Yahuah, risking her life for her people with a heart fully surrendered to divine purpose.

- **The Proverbs 31 Woman (Proverbs 31:30):** She embodies reverence through her diligence, wisdom, and fear of Yahuah, which is the root of her virtuous character.

Living in the Fear of Yahuah Today

For the modern biblical woman, cultivating reverence for Yahuah requires intentionality. This means:

1. **Prioritizing Time in the Word:** Meditating on Scripture strengthens her understanding of Yahuah's will.

2. **Cultivating a Prayerful Life:** Seeking Yahuah in daily matters fosters spiritual intimacy.

3. **Living in Holiness:** Guarding her actions, speech, and thoughts reflects her commitment to righteousness.

4. **Teaching and Leading by Example:** Instilling reverence

in her household ensures a legacy of faith.

5. **Surrounding Herself with Godly Counsel:** She seeks the wisdom of righteous women and elders to guide her walk in truth **(Titus 2:3-5).**

The art of fear is not about living in hesitation or insecurity; it is about moving with certainty and divine confidence. A woman who fears Yahuah does not waver because she knows He upholds her. She does not seek validation from the world because she is already affirmed by The Creator. She walks in a sacred dance with her Creator, every step guided by His wisdom, every word flowing from a heart that reveres Him. Her reverence is not restrictive but liberating, positioning her as a vessel for divine purpose. As she deepens her awe and respect for Elohim. She becomes a light to those around her, reflecting His wisdom, love, and righteousness in all she does. May we all learn to embrace the art of holy fear, walking in reverence, wisdom, and unshakable faith.

Selah Moment:

Take a moment to reflect on your relationship with Yahuah. Do you approach Him with the reverence and awe He deserves? In what areas of your life can you grow in honoring Him more? Pray for a heart that delights in His commandments, a mind that seeks His wisdom, and a spirit that remains steadfast in His presence. Remember, reverence is not about fear that repels but about love that draws near.

"She Knows Who She Answers To"

She walks with purpose, head held high,
Not swayed by whispers, nor tempted to lie.
Her steps are measured, her path is clear,
For the voice of Yah is all she hears.

Not fear that binds, nor dread that chains,
But deep reverence, where wisdom reigns.
She bows in awe, yet stands so tall,
For she serves the One who rules it all.

Her words are guarded, her hands are pure,
Her faith is firm, her stance is sure.
No reckless steps, no aimless way,
She moves with Yah; she does not stray.

The world may mock, may plot, may pry,
But she won't fold, she won't comply.
For she fears Yah more than man,
And in His purpose, she will stand.

She knows Who sees, she knows Who guides,
And in His shadow, she abides.
A daughter crowned, refined, made new—
She walks in fear, and knows how to draw near.

Redefining Helpmeet

I always pictured myself as a helpmeet—you know, cooking, cleaning, decorating the house, creating peace and beauty. That was my vision. But when I began to truly seek TMH's definition of a helpmeet... let's just say, I was deeply humbled.

*We tend to romanticize marriage—the beautiful wedding, the fairytale life, the happily-ever-after. But **Ezer**—the Hebrew word for helpmeet—is so much deeper than domestic duties and dreamy expectations. It carries weight, responsibility, and a level of spiritual maturity I wasn't prepared for at first.*

*What I didn't realize is that becoming a true helpmeet starts before marriage. **It begins in singleness.** It begins with saving yourself, learning how to govern your spirit, and becoming a wise counselor. Before I could ever be called a woman of virtue, **I had to first pursue wisdom—and then walk in it**.*

I couldn't help or support something I didn't understand. I couldn't be a leader's wife if I hadn't first learned how to counsel, advise, and walk beside a leader. That meant I had to develop within myself the very traits I would one day be called to support.

This realization drove me back to the foundation—knowing Yah and understanding the role He created me to fulfill. I needed to know what I was built for so that I wouldn't be deceived like Eve, wandering outside of my divine assignment.

And so, I began the work—becoming the woman who reflects His wisdom, not just the woman who keeps a clean house.

To be continued...

CHAPTER 3 THE ART OF BEING AN ALLY (EZER)

"She's, his rib."

From the very beginning, Yahuah designed woman with a distinct and powerful role—one that is often misunderstood and diminished in modern interpretations. The word "helpmeet" (**Ezer Knegdo**) first appears in Genesis when Yahuah declares, *"It is not good that the man should be alone; I will make him a help meet for him."* **(Genesis 2:18)**

In Hebrew, *"Ezer"* means "help" but not in a secondary or subservient way. It is the same word used to describe Yahuah as the helper of Israel **(Psalm 121:1-2)**. *"Knegdo"* means "corresponding to" or "alongside," showing that the woman was created as a counterpart, not a lesser being. This role is not about servitude, but about partnership—standing as a pillar of support, wisdom, and strength in faith.

Eve (*Chawwah,* **meaning "life"**) was the first woman, the mother of all living. Created from Adam's side—not his head to rule over him, nor his feet to be trampled by him—she was formed to stand beside him. However, the fall of man brought distortion to her role. Instead of acting as a wise counselor, Eve was deceived by the serpent **(Genesis 3:1-6)**.

This moment in history is often used to discredit the wisdom and discernment of women, yet it should serve as a reminder of why a woman's spiritual awareness and guidance are crucial. Had she sought Yahuah before acting, the course of history may have been different. A righteous helpmate does not move impulsively but seeks divine wisdom before making decisions that impact her household.

In Hebraic tradition, the role of a wife was more than domestic. She was an integral part of the family's spiritual life, a keeper of Torah within the home, and often a businesswoman, as seen in the Proverbs 31 woman. A wife in biblical times was responsible for teaching the children, managing the household, and even handling trade and commerce **(Proverbs 31:16, 24)**. She does not operate independently of her husband but works in unity, enhancing the family's spiritual and material well-being.

- **Sarah:** A woman of deep faith who partnered with Abraham in the covenant promises **(Genesis 17:15-16, Hebrews 11:11)**.

- **Rebekah:** A woman of discernment who played a key role in fulfilling divine prophecy concerning Jacob and Esau **(Genesis 27:5-13)**.

- **Deborah:** A wife, prophetess, and judge, showing that being a helpmate does not mean silence or passivity, but active spiritual leadership **(Judges 4:4-9)**.

The Power of Partnership

Being a helpmate does not mean losing one's identity. It means being an active participant in a divine mission. A woman is called to be the heart of her home, a nurturer of faith, and a wise counselor. This role requires:

1. **Spiritual Strength:** A woman should seek to be deeply rooted in Torah, walking in discernment and wisdom.

2. **Faithful Counsel:** Just as Abigail advised David with

wisdom **(1 Samuel 25:23-31)**, a helpmate should offer sound advice, keeping her household aligned with righteousness.

3. **Encouragement and Support:** A woman strengthens her husband through prayer and encouragement, lifting him when he is weary **(Ecclesiastes 4:9-12)**.

4. **Teaching and Legacy:** She imparts knowledge of Yahuah to her children and community, ensuring that generations after her walk in truth **(Deuteronomy 6:6-7)**.

A biblical helpmate is more than a companion; she is a spiritual force in the home and beyond. Her role encompasses:

1. **Encouragement & Support:** She strengthens her husband in faith and righteous living **(Ecclesiastes 4:9-10)**.

2. **Intercession & Prayer:** She prays fervently for her husband, children, and household **(Proverbs 31:30)**.

3. **Wisdom & Discernment:** She provides insight and counsel, helping her husband make godly decisions **(Proverbs 14:1)**.

4. **Cultivating Peace & Order:** She sets the spiritual atmosphere in the home, ensuring it remains a place of shalom **(Titus 2:4-5)**.

5. **Nurturing & Teaching:** She raises children in the ways of Yahuah, passing down wisdom and faith **(Deuteronomy 6:6-7)**

The Beauty of the Helpmate's Calling

A woman who embraces her role as a helpmate walks in divine purpose. She is not a servant, but a co-laborer in righteousness. She is not silenced, but a voice of wisdom. She is not weak, but a strong and faithful steward of the home and community. Her role is one of power, grace, and divine purpose—designed by Yahuah to reflect His heart in the earth.

As you continue this journey, ask yourself: How can I embody the role of an "*Ezer Knegdo*" in my life? May Yahuah strengthen and guide you as you walk in the art of being a helpmate.

The role of a wife was seen as one of honor, and she was entrusted with the well-being of her household.

- **The Woman as the Keeper of the Home:** In Hebraic tradition, the wife was entrusted with maintaining the holiness of the household. This was not limited to domestic duties but extended to spiritual leadership within the home.

- **The Role in Community:** Women participated in community gatherings, worship, and teaching. Supporting not only their husbands but also the broader faith community.

Selah Moment:

Take a moment to reflect: How do you view the role of a helpmate? Have you ever seen it as a limitation rather than a divine calling? In what ways can you strengthen your role as a spiritual partner in your home and community? Pray for wisdom and discernment, that you may walk in the fullness of your role as a helpmate. Ask Yahuah to shape you into a woman of faith, wisdom, and strength, standing firmly in the role He has ordained for you.

"To Stand Beside to Rise Within"

I was not made to dim my flame,
Nor walk behind in silent shame.
But fashioned firm, with wisdom deep,
A garden soul, designed to keep.

A helpmeet—not in shadow's stay,
But in the dawn to light the way.
Not less, not weak, not second best,
But strength adorned in humble dress.

I stand beside—not in control,
But yoked in love, with heart made whole.
To lift when burden bows the head,
To intercede, to pray instead.

When purpose calls, I do not flee,
For purpose lives and breathes in me.
Not just to serve, but also see—
The man, the plan, the prophecy.

My counsel comes not sharp with pride,
But like still waters, sanctified.
My hands bring healing, not disdain,
My words are oil that soothe the pain.

A crown, a covering, a root,
A tree that bears enduring fruit.
Not just to build, but to believe,
To guard, to labor, and conceive.

For I am she, divinely placed,
With sacred steps and quiet grace.
To be an ally, bold and true—
Not just for him, but for You too.

Learning How To Read The Room

Remember when I mentioned not wanting to be deceived like Eve? Well, learning the art of discernment and prudence was truly the icing on the cake of my spiritual development.

One thing I've always struggled with is people who can't read the room. But Yah, in His wisdom, showed me that I couldn't just expect others to have discernment—I had to master it myself. Meditation became my training ground. It sharpened my ability to observe, to sit still, and to perceive beyond the surface. I began to understand that what we see with our eyes is nothing compared to what's happening in the spirit realm, simultaneously and silently.

This sensitivity taught me how to "try the spirit by the spirit," But to do that, my own spirit had to be alert, submitted, and attuned to Yah's voice. I had to know when to speak, how to speak, and most importantly—when to remain silent and avoid walking straight into the enemy's trap.

That's where prudence came in. I like to call prudence discernment's modesty. It taught me tact—how to move with grace, caution, and intention. It made me strategic. It wasn't just about knowing something was wrong or right, but understanding how to respond in wisdom, and when to act in love.

This journey began to build a confidence in me that was rooted not in self, but in Yah's direction. I no longer leaned on my own understanding. Confusion had no place because my steps were ordered. When I entered a room, I let my spirit enter first—quiet, open, and ready for Yah to reveal whatever I needed to see.

I wasn't walking in with an agenda anymore—I was simply a vessel, willing and prepared, fully trusting in Yah's lead and becoming a sure decision maker.

To be continued...

CHAPTER 4 THE ART OF DISCERNMENT AND PRUDENCE

"She peeps game and reads the room"

One of the most powerful, yet often underestimated, gifts a woman carries is the ability to "read the room." This is not just about noticing who is present but understanding the unspoken, sensing the shifts in energy, and discerning what is truly happening beyond words. This ability allows a woman to walk in wisdom, ensuring she responds to situations with grace, strategy, and intention.

A wise woman pays attention to more than just what is said—she notices body language, tone, and the underlying atmosphere. Imagine walking into a gathering where tension is thick in the air —perhaps a disagreement just occurred. A woman attuned to her surroundings notices the small details: the way someone's arms are crossed, the shift in someone's tone, or the nervous glances exchanged. Instead of diving into the conversation unguarded, she first discerns the atmosphere. Should she offer comforting words? Stay silent? Change the subject to defuse tension? This skill is invaluable not just in social settings but also in marriage, motherhood, business, and leadership.

A mother, for example, knows when her child has had a difficult day just by their posture or lack of words. A wife senses when her husband needs encouragement before he even speaks. A woman who can read the emotional and spiritual temperature of a room and act accordingly carries the ability to bring peace and insight where needed. This sensitivity is not meant to make a woman anxious, but rather, to equip her to act appropriately—whether in silence, through intercession, or by speaking when necessary.

In Hebraic culture, women have always been entrusted with keen discernment. Take, for example, **Abigail** in 1 Samuel 25. She observed the folly of her husband, Nabal, and wisely interceded to prevent calamity from befalling her household. She read the tension in the atmosphere, understood the potential consequences, and acted with wisdom and humility.

Another example is **Deborah**, the prophetess and judge (Judges 4). She had the ability to discern the times and lead Israel with both strength and grace. Her awareness of Yahuah's timing and her wisdom in guiding Barak into battle were vital in securing victory for her people. She saw beyond the present moment and into the greater spiritual picture.

In Hebraic culture, women were not passive observers but active participants who used their discernment to shape history. Two prime examples of this are **Sarah and Rebekah**, both of whom demonstrated keen awareness and wisdom in their ability to read situations and act accordingly.

Sarah: Discerning Destiny

Sarah, the matriarch of Israel, understood the gravity of protecting the covenant Yahuah had established through Isaac. When she noticed Ishmael mocking Isaac **(Genesis 21:9-10)**, she did not dismiss it as mere sibling rivalry. She discerned the deeper implications—an opposition to Isaac's role in the covenant. She urged Abraham to send Hagar and Ishmael away, a decision Yahuah Himself affirmed **(Genesis 21:12)**. Sarah's ability to read the room ensured the covenant's integrity.

Rebekah: Perceiving Spiritual Authority

Rebekah displayed profound discernment when she noticed the stark differences between her twin sons, Esau and Jacob. She walked in the confidence given through receiving the prophecy. She recognized that Jacob was the one fit to carry the blessing and understood that Isaac's failing eyesight did not only symbolize physical blindness but also spiritual blindness to Esau's true nature. Acting with urgency, she guided Jacob in securing the blessing **(Genesis 27)**. Her wisdom ensured that the covenant promise was handed to the son who would honor it.

Practical Applications in Daily Life

1. **In the Home** – A woman should be able to sense when peace is disrupted in her household. Perhaps an argument is brewing, or maybe her family is under spiritual attack. Instead of reacting emotionally, she can step back, pray, and address the situation with wisdom.

2. **In the Community** – Whether in fellowship, business, or casual gatherings, a woman who reads the room can discern who needs encouragement, when to speak, and when to remain silent. She is the one who notices when a sister is feeling out of place and makes her feel welcomed.

3. **In Marriage** – Sometimes, a husband may not express his concerns verbally, but a discerning wife picks up on his silent burdens. Instead of demanding answers, she can support him through prayer, a kind word, or simply offering him space to process.

4. **With Children** – Mothers often sense when something is troubling their child. Instead of dismissing it, they can gently inquire, offer comfort, or pray over them, strengthening the child's trust and security.

A woman who hones her ability to read the room becomes a

source of strength in her home and community. Here are some ways to develop this skill:

5. **Stay Close to Yahuah** – The more we seek Him, the clearer our vision becomes. Prayer and scripture study sharpen our spiritual senses.

6. **Deepen Your Knowledge of Scripture** – The Word of Yahuah is the ultimate standard of truth. A woman who meditates on the Word will recognize deception when it arises **(Hebrews 4:12)**.

7. **Practice Active Listening** – Pay attention to what is being said—and what isn't. Often, body language and tone reveal more than words.

8. **Listen More Than You Speak** - Observe, ask questions, and seek deeper understanding before reacting.

9. **Seek the Ruach HaKodesh** – Ask Yahuah for discernment before making decisions, just as our foremothers did. Spiritual discernment comes through the Holy Spirit's guidance. Prayer and fasting sharpen one's ability to hear Yahuah's voice **(James 1:5)**.

10. **Observe Without Judging** - Rather than jumping to conclusions, take time to understand the dynamics at play. – Yahshua taught that a tree is known by its fruit **(Matthew 7:16)**. A woman must watch carefully to see if words and actions align with righteousness.

11. **Respond with Wisdom, Not Emotion** – A woman who reads the room well does not react impulsively but moves with grace and purpose.

12. **Deepen Your Knowledge of Scripture** – The Word of Yahuah is the ultimate standard of truth. A woman who meditates on the Word will recognize deception when it arises (Hebrews 4:12).

13. **Practice Spiritual Stillness** – In a noisy world, taking time for silence and reflection allows a woman to process and evaluate situations with clarity **(Psalm 46:10)**.

14. **Trust But Verify** – Not all that glitters is gold. Things are not always what they seem. A prudent woman verifies the authenticity of teachings, leaders, and situations before fully embracing them **(Proverbs 14:15)**.

15. **Trust Your Spirit, Not Just Your Eyes** –. Ask Yahuah for wisdom before making decisions, especially in relationships and leadership roles.

16. **Surround Yourself with Wise Counsel** – The people we listen to influence how we see the world. Wise, godly friends and mentors help refine our discernment.

This is the essence of discernment and prudence. It is not about being suspicious of everything, but about seeing beyond the surface, aligning with the Spirit of Yahuah, and making choices that protect and uplift. A discerning woman understands that not everything is as it seems. She seeks wisdom from Yahuah, knowing that her ability to navigate life depends on spiritual clarity.

Proverbs 3:5-6 reminds us: *"Trust in Yahuah with all thine heart; and lean not unto thine own understanding. In all thy ways acknowledge Him, and He shall direct thy paths."* Discernment is the ability to perceive truth in a world filled with deception, to separate what is good from what merely looks good.

Scripture warns us to test all things: *"Beloved, believe not every spirit, but try the spirits whether they are of Elohim: because many false prophets are gone out into the world."* **(1 John 4:1)**. Without discernment, one can easily fall into deception, mistaking appearances for reality. A wise woman does not act solely on emotions but seeks understanding through prayer and divine wisdom.

Prudence: Acting Wisely in Decision-Making

Discernment is not just about recognizing truth; it is about applying wisdom in decision-making. Prudence helps a woman know when to speak and when to remain silent, when to act and when to wait.

A woman who masters the art of discernment walks in strength and confidence. She does not waver in confusion but stands firm in spiritual clarity. As you grow in this gift, remember: Yahuah has given you the ability to read the room, to sense His guidance, and to make decisions that align with His perfect will. Lean into that wisdom, and let it lead you in every area of your life.

Selah Moment:

> *Take a moment to reflect on how Yahuah is sharpening your discernment for the journey ahead. Have you encountered situations where discernment could have prevented hardship? How can you better cultivate prudence in your daily life? Think about a time when you discerned something others didn't see. How did that moment shape your path? Ask Yahuah to sharpen your discernment, helping you to see with spiritual eyes and move with wisdom.*

"From The Lens Of The Discerning Soul"

I enter not with thunder's pace,
But with the hush of holy grace.
Eyes like lamps, spirit tuned,
I read the air; I scan the room.

Not every silence is the same,
Not every smile speaks one name.
The heart may hide, the face may lie,
But wisdom hears the inward cry.

I watch the flow, the subtle cues,
The shifting tone, the worn-out shoes.
The laugh too loud, the glance too brief—
All signs etched deep in silent grief.

Not all are called to speak aloud,
Some minister without the crowd.
A touch, a nod, a timely move,
Can shift the space and softly soothe.

I do not rush to take up space,
But fill what's void with quiet grace.
Not to perform or to presume—
But master stillness in the room.

For presence is a sacred art,
To feel what's hid inside the heart.
To be aware, yet not assume—
This is the gift: to read the room.

Becoming Virtue/Chayil

Chayil—well, that's kind of my name...but learning Hebrew gave that word a whole new weight I wasn't ready for.

In mainstream religion, "virtuous" is often portrayed like a checklist—be kind, dress modestly, smile, serve, repeat. But when I began digging deeper, studying the language and spirit behind the word, I quickly realized it was far more than a list. Virtue isn't about doing—it's about becoming.

The Hebrew perspective revealed that to walk as a capable woman —a woman of valor, strength, and moral excellence—requires deep inner work. It demanded a daily posture of humility and vulnerability before the Creator. Not just when I felt weak, but especially when I thought I was strong.

I had to learn how to exchange my strength for His—the kind of strength called Gevurah, which isn't just power, but disciplined, spiritual might. I had to train myself to draw from Yah's well, not just my own reserves.

My morals, my instincts, my perspectives had to be surrendered—over and over—until they were in full alignment with His standards. This wasn't about being flawless; it was about being faithful to the process.

And as I matured, I learned the balance: when to stand firm and fight —spiritually and physically—and when to step back and let Yah take over completely. Sometimes virtue looks like action, and sometimes it looks like restraint. Either way, it always looks like obedience.

I wasn't just wearing the name "Chayil." I was being called to become her.

To be continued...

CHAPTER 5 THE ART OF VIRTUE

"She walkin' right."

A virtuous woman is not merely someone who does good deeds—she embodies *righteousness, integrity, and moral excellence*. Virtue is not a *performance* but a *way of life*, deeply rooted in the Torah and the fear of Yahuah. Her character speaks louder than her words, and her presence exudes the light of righteousness.

In Hebrew, the word for virtue is *"Chayil"* (,(חיל meaning *strength, valor,* and *moral excellence.* **Proverbs 31:10** describes the virtuous woman as *"Eshet Chayil,"* a woman of strength and honor. Virtue is not about perfection, but about the pursuit of righteousness, consistently choosing what is right even when it is difficult. The virtuous woman does not shy away from challenges but confronts them with *wisdom, courage,* and *grace.* Her heart is committed to seeking righteousness in every situation, demonstrating that true virtue is not about flawless execution but the integrity to always choose what aligns with the will of Yahuah.

Her strength is not only physical but spiritual as well. She is a woman who stands firm in her faith, with a heart anchored in the teachings of the Torah. In moments of adversity, her foundation in righteousness becomes the bedrock upon which she stands. Her strength is evident in her ability to withstand the storms of life while remaining unshaken in her devotion to truth and justice. She is a light in her community, a beacon of moral clarity, and a model of righteousness for others to follow.

The virtuous woman, in all her strength and wisdom, understands that her actions must reflect her inner integrity. She lives by the words of the Torah, allowing its truths to guide her thoughts and decisions. She does not seek external validation but is deeply rooted in the approval of Yahuah, knowing that it is His will she seeks to fulfill. Her *actions,* motivated by *love, humility,* and the *fear of Yahuah*, radiate a quiet yet powerful strength that speaks volumes in her home, community, and beyond.

Virtue, then, is not a one-time act but a continuous journey of growth, learning, and refinement. A virtuous woman does not settle for what is easy or popular; instead, she pursues righteousness with unwavering commitment. She understands that her worth is not measured by the world's standards but by her faithfulness to Yahuah's ways. This pursuit of righteousness shapes her character, her relationships, and her legacy, creating a life that honors Yahuah and impacts those around her in profound ways.

Ultimately, the virtuous woman is a reflection of the heart of Yahuah, embodying His strength, wisdom, and love in everything she does. Her life is a testimony to the power of virtue, shining as a witness of the transformative effect that living in accordance with the Torah can have on one's character, relationships, and legacy.

A virtuous woman:

- **Speaks with kindness and truth** – She does not gossip or tear others down **(Proverbs 31:26)**.

- **Walks in righteousness** – Her actions align with Torah, and she pursues justice and mercy **(Micah 6:8)**.

- **Honors her commitments** – She is trustworthy and keeps her word **(Psalm 15:4)**.

- **Guards her purity** – She respects herself and others, understanding that virtue is both inward and outward **(1 Timothy 2:9-10)**.

Selah Moment:

What areas of my life need more integrity and righteousness? Do my words and actions align with the Torah's definition of virtue? How can I cultivate virtue in my daily life? Pause. Reflect. Seek Yahuah's wisdom in strengthening your walk in virtue.

"The Quiet Crown"

Virtue is not loud nor proud,
It doesn't beg to please the crowd.
It walks in truth, with garments clean,
Unshaken by what's felt or seen.

It is the hush before the storm,
The warmth that keeps the spirit warm.
A steadfast heart, a tempered tongue,
A song unsung, but deeply sung.

It does not boast, it does not strive,
Yet gives all dead things strength to rise.
It bends, but never breaks or flees,
Rooted like ancient olive trees.

It's in what no one else will say,
The turning from the easy way.
It's holding peace when wronged and tried,
And choosing honor over pride.

Virtue is the oil refined,
The fragrance of a holy mind.
The posture of a yielded soul,
That walks in purpose, pure and whole.

This is the art—to guard the flame,
To wear your worth, not chase a name.
To be the truth in a world grown numb—
The light that tells the King, "I've come."

The Crown Of Wisdom

This is the crown I long to wear—especially in my old age.

Everything Yah has been revealing to me in this season feels like a deposit into a spiritual bank account of wisdom. It's not always flashy, and it rarely comes quickly. But it builds—quietly, steadily, and deeply. We often speak of King Solomon as the wisest man to walk the earth, but we sometimes overlook why—the years of peace he experienced, the diverse cultures he ruled, the countless decisions he had to make, and the people who tested and activated the wisdom given to him. His wisdom wasn't just gifted—it was stewarded.

That's what I'm learning. Wisdom is layered. It's a divine compilation of life lessons, spiritual revelations, hard choices, quiet observations, and surrendered understanding. It's timeless. It doesn't age—it expands. It reshapes your perspectives, sharpens your discernment, and humbles you in the vastness of Yah's greatness and the smallness of your own understanding.

In the beginning, wisdom can feel like a challenge—so many choices, so many voices. But the book of Proverbs becomes a lamp in the fog, gently guiding you to choose life, over and over again. Eventually, wisdom becomes sweet—like honey to the soul. And when it's mishandled or lost, it can be devastating.

That's why I constantly remind myself: Stay focused. Just as Solomon —so rich in wisdom—lost his way through compromise, so can I. Wisdom is rare. Priceless. And once you've tasted it, you realize it's not just a tool; it's a crown. One worth guarding like treasure. One that reflects not just your growth, but Yah's glory.

To be continued....

CHAPTER 6 THE ART OF WISDOM

"She got that old soul knowledge."

Wisdom is a woman's crown. It is what distinguishes the foolish from the righteous, the immature from the discerning. A woman of wisdom listens before she *speaks, discerns, acts,* and *will always seek* The Most High's guidance in all things.

In Hebrew, wisdom is *Chakmah* ((חָכְמָה, a deep, spiritual understanding that comes from Yahuah. **Proverbs 4:7** declares, *"Wisdom is the principal thing; therefore, get wisdom: and with all thy getting get understanding."* Wisdom is not simply intelligence —it is applied knowledge rooted in divine truth. Her life reflects His wisdom, flowing through her in her relationships, decisions, and actions. Wisdom is more than a quality, it is an essence, something that defines and shapes her. Here, wisdom is not just an abstract concept, it's a pursuit, a treasure to seek and cultivate.

But to understand *chokhmah* in its full richness, it helps to explore its connection to the Sefirot, the divine emanations in Kabbalistic tradition that describe how Yahuah's attributes flow into creation. Specifically, *chokhmah* is associated with the energy of divine insight, the initial spark of wisdom. It is often considered the first step in understanding, the flash of inspiration that comes from Yahuah, but it is incomplete without the counterpart—*binah* (בִּינָה), which is understanding, discernment, and the ability to process and integrate that insight.

Together, *chokhmah* and *binah* represent a balance between intuitive wisdom and practical application. A woman of wisdom, therefore, is someone who not only receives the spark of *chokhmah*—the deep insight from Yahuah—but who also cultivates *binah*, the ability to comprehend and apply that insight in a way that brings peace and righteousness into her life and the lives of those around her.

Chokmah and Binah in a Woman's Life

When we consider *chokhmah* and *binah* together, we see that wisdom is both a gift and a practice. The energy of *chokhmah* is like a divine spark—an illumination of the heart and mind from Yahuah. *Binah,* however, represents the nurturing, cultivating energy of a woman who processes that spark, makes sense of it, and transforms it into something practical, something that can be applied in real life.

In the life of a woman, these two forces work hand-in-hand. Her intuition, her *chokhmah*, leads her to the right paths, while her *binah* gives her the clarity to walk them. A woman who walks in these divine energies is a woman who reflects the wisdom of Yahuah in every action, in every decision, and in every relationship.

In Hebraic thought, **Chokmah** (wisdom) and **Binah** (understanding) represent two essential aspects of divine energy, often described as masculine and feminine, respectively. Here are some real-life examples that highlight the difference between these energies:

1. In a Relationship:

- **Chokmah (Masculine Energy):** A man might initiate a relationship or propose a new idea, bringing the spark of insight or direction. This energy is about taking action, starting projects, and offering leadership. In a relationship, Chokmah is the energy that takes initiative, the one who might lead with vision and ideas.

- **Binah (Feminine Energy):** The woman, embodying Binah, nurtures, understands, and helps develop the initial idea. She listens, processes, and refines it, drawing on her deep capacity to understand the nuances and underlying needs of both the relationship and the idea. She provides structure, cultivating wisdom with patience, care, and intuitive insight.

To bring it full circle, the man (Chokmah) carries the vision, but the woman (Binah) holds the details of the plan. Together, they complete the vision, each fulfilling a unique and complementary role.

In partnership, they are a unified force, as the scriptures declare:

- *"Two are better than one; because they have a good reward for their labour."* **(Ecclesiastes 4:9)** – Together, the masculine energy of Chokmah and the feminine energy of Binah complete the task, each contributing their strengths to fulfill the vision.

2. In the Process of Creation:

- **Chokmah (Masculine Energy):** Chokmah is the seed of an idea or the initial flash of inspiration. Think of it as a creative impulse or the initial plan. In a business venture, it's the entrepreneur's spark to start a new product or company. This energy is more about the **"what"** and **"why"** of creation, setting a vision and determining the direction.

- **Binah (Feminine Energy):** Binah takes that initial idea and nurtures it, shaping it into a concrete reality. In the same business venture, Binah is the strategy and

50

planning phase, where the concept is carefully thought through and developed into a practical, workable model. It's the **"how"** the implementation, refinement, and deeper understanding of the plan.

3. In Problem-Solving:

- **Chokmah (Masculine Energy):** In a problem-solving scenario, Chokmah is the first response, the moment of clarity when you come up with an insight or solution. It's often fast, direct, and intuitive. It's like the sudden "aha!" moment when a person sees the solution to a problem clearly.

- **Binah (Feminine Energy):** Once Chokmah brings forward the solution, Binah steps in to examine it from every angle. Binah is analytical, examining the depth of the solution, considering all variables, and ensuring that it will be effective in the long term. Binah brings clarity, structure, and understanding to the initial idea, considering the impact and practicality.

4. In Parenting:

- **Chokmah (Masculine Energy):** The father may provide the initial guidance, principles, and direction for the child. He is the one who sets the boundaries and pushes the child to grow and achieve their potential. His role is to encourage and challenge, often bringing a sense of purpose and vision into the child's life.

- **Binah (Feminine Energy):** The mother, embodying Binah, nourishes, supports, and deeply understands the child's emotional and psychological needs. She intuitively understands when something is wrong and helps the child process their feelings. Her energy is focused on providing a safe environment for growth and developing emotional intelligence, teaching through empathy and connection.

5. In Spirituality:

- **Chokmah (Masculine Energy):** In spiritual practice, Chokmah represents the divine masculine energy, which is the direct revelation or moment of connection with the divine. It's the flash of insight or the vision that gives one a deeper understanding of purpose or truth. It often manifests as wisdom that leads toward higher consciousness.

- **Binah (Feminine Energy):** Binah represents the feminine energy that takes that divine spark and nurtures it into a personal, lived experience. It is the practice of integrating that wisdom into the soul, understanding its application, and embodying it in the heart. Binah works to bring the lofty concepts of Chokmah down into the everyday, grounding them in reality.

A woman who walks in wisdom does so in several key ways:

1. **She seeks Yahuah first**
   Before making decisions, whether large or small, she turns to Yahuah in prayer and study of His word. **James 1:5** encourages us, *"If any of you lack wisdom, let him ask of Yahuah, that giveth to all men liberally, and upbraideth not; and it shall be given him."* She trusts that Yahuah's wisdom will guide her path, so she humbly seeks His guidance before acting.

2. **She listens more than she speaks**
   In **Proverbs 17:27-28,** it says, *"He that hath knowledge spareth his words: and a man of understanding is of an excellent spirit. Even a fool, when he holdeth his peace, is counted wise: and he that shutteth his lips is esteemed a man of understanding."* A woman of wisdom understands that silence and listening are key

components of discernment. She does not rush to speak but instead listens intently, allowing time for understanding to settle before responding.

3. **She builds her home with wisdom**
A wise woman creates an environment where peace, understanding, and righteousness flourish. **Proverbs 14:1** reminds us, *"Every wise woman buildeth her house: but the foolish plucketh it down with her hands."* Her wisdom is not only seen in her decisions but also in how she fosters an atmosphere of love, respect, and tranquility in her home. She nurtures those around her with her understanding and guidance.

In essence, Chokmah is like the initial spark or fire that begins the process, while Binah is the fertile ground that nurtures and shapes that initial energy into something meaningful, tangible, and enduring. Both energies are essential for a balanced life and creation, with *Chokmah bringing direction and impulse and Binah providing understanding, depth, and manifestation.*

Selah Moment:

- *Do I seek wisdom before reacting, or do I act impulsively? Am I allowing Yahuah to guide my decisions, especially in moments of uncertainty or difficulty? How can I cultivate more wisdom in my daily life, embracing both chokhmah and binah?*

Take a moment to pause. Reflect. Seek Yahuah's wisdom in all things. Allow His wisdom to be your guide and your strength, nurturing your understanding, so that you might walk in righteousness and build a life full of peace, discernment, and divine purpose.

"Wisdom"

A woman of wisdom, radiant and true,
With Chokmah's vision, she sees it through.
Her mind a beacon, sharp and bright,
Guiding the lost with holy light.

Chokmah whispers, the spark of fire,
In her soul, the dreams aspire.
A flash of insight, a bold decree,
The path ahead, for all to see.

But Binah, her heart, a gentle guide,
Molds the vision, stands by her side.
In silence, she deepens every plan,
With quiet strength, she understands.

She builds with care, her wisdom's hands,
Crafting the future on steady sands.
With each small step, the vision grows,
Nurtured by grace, it softly flows.

Her wisdom, a dance of both fire and earth,
Chokmah and Binah, giving life birth.
A woman of wisdom, both fierce and kind,
With clarity's light and love intertwined.

The Servant's Mirror

Remember that humility and vulnerability I mentioned with wisdom? I quickly realized I would need both even more when it came to **servanthood***.*

The deeper I walked in obedience to Yah, the stronger my desire grew to help others. It became clear that everything I once lacked—mentorship, sisterhood, someone to support me when I was struggling—wasn't just a wound to be healed, but a calling. I was being shaped to become the very person I once needed to show up for me.

Every gift, resource, witty idea, and purposeful spark within me wasn't just for me—it was a catalyst, a vessel Yah designed to serve others in the capacity He created me for.

And the beautiful thing about true service? Your needs are met while you're meeting the needs of others. TMH pours back into you, not just with material things, but in deep, soul-level restoration. Serving children taught me patience, revealed unhealed parts of my inner child, and helped me reparent myself. Serving mothers prepared me to be a better mother, a more compassionate sister, and gave me insight to guard my marriage from generational patterns I'd seen.

Servanthood became my training ground. It sharpened my wisdom, confronted my triggers, and broke my selfish tendencies. It showed me that community isn't optional—it's necessary. We need mirrors, and often, those mirrors are found in the people we serve.

But that meant I had to leave my comfort zone. I had to leave my house, engage with people, learn how to communicate, and choose selflessness over self-protection. Only then could I become blameless—not in perfection, but in posture.

Servanthood isn't about being seen. It's about becoming whole enough to see others and love them through Yah's lens.

CHAPTER 7 THE ART OF SERVANTHOOD

"She the backbone."

A righteous woman is the backbone of her home, her family, and her community. Through her servanthood, she holds everything together, ensuring that love, order, and wisdom flow throughout her household. Servanthood is not about weakness but about strength—strength in humility, grace, and selflessness. A biblical woman's servanthood is her power, a gift that elevates her and those around her.

Servanthood is deeply embedded in the fabric of righteous womanhood. It is the act of putting others before oneself, of embodying love through action, and of strengthening those she serves. In the world, servanthood is often mistaken for subjugation, but in the Kingdom, it is the highest calling—one that shapes character, refines the heart, and manifests the wisdom of Yah.

Yahshua Himself declared, *"Whoever wants to be great among you must be your servant"* **(Matthew 20:26)**. A righteous woman understands that greatness is found not in lording over others but in lifting them up.

The Scriptures offer profound examples of women whose humility and service positioned them for divine favor and influence:

- **Rebekah (Genesis 24:17-20):** When Abraham's servant

sought a wife for Isaac, he prayed for a woman who would offer water not just to him but also to his camels. Rebekah, without hesitation, drew water for both, demonstrating a heart of hospitality and service. Her selflessness set her apart, marking her as the chosen one for Isaac.

- **Ruth (Ruth 2:2-7, 3:10-11):** Ruth's dedication to Naomi and her willingness to glean in the fields with humility displayed a servanthood that caught the eye of Boaz. Her service was not out of obligation but out of love and honor. Her heart of service positioned her in the lineage of King David and ultimately, the Messiah.

- **Abigail (1 Samuel 25:18-35):** When her foolish husband, Nabal, disrespected David, Abigail acted swiftly. She prepared provisions and approached David with wisdom and humility, preventing unnecessary bloodshed. Her servanthood was paired with discernment, revealing that a woman who serves wisely preserves the house.

- **Mary, the mother of Yahshua (Luke 1:38, John 2:1-5):** Mary's willingness to submit to The Most High's will was the ultimate act of servanthood. Her response, *"Behold the handmaid of the Lord; be it unto me according to thy word"* **(Luke 1:38)**, embodies the humility required of every woman who walks in divine purpose.

Self-Serving Ambition vs. Selfless Service

In contrast to servanthood, self-serving ambition leads to destruction. The world glorifies self-promotion, but The Most High calls for selflessness. Consider the example of Queen Vashti **(Esther 1:10-12)**, who, though positioned as a queen, refused to honor her husband's request, leading to her removal. In contrast, Esther, with wisdom and humility, risked her life to save her people **(Esther 4:16)**. One sought self, the other sought service—the difference in their outcomes speaks volumes.

A righteous woman does not seek her own elevation but trusts that Yah will exalt her in due time **(1 Peter 5:6)**. When a woman serves, she plants seeds of honor that will yield a harvest of favor.

Humility refines a woman's character. It keeps her heart pure and her motives righteous. A woman who walks in humility is teachable, discerning, and filled with wisdom. She understands that servanthood is not about losing herself but about becoming the vessel through which Yah's light shines.

A servant-hearted woman is not easily shaken. She operates in peace because she knows her strength comes from The Most High. She is like the Proverbs 31 woman, whose hands work diligently, whose words bring kindness, and whose presence establishes security in her household **(Proverbs 31:10-31)**.

Applying Servanthood in Daily Life

1. **Serving in the Home** – A woman builds her home through love, patience, and care **(Proverbs 14:1)**. Whether it is nurturing her children, honoring her husband, or tending to daily responsibilities, she serves with joy, knowing that her work is unto Yah.

2. **Serving in the Community** – Just as Dorcas **(Acts 9:36)** was known for her good works, a righteous woman extends her hands to the poor, uplifts those in need, and reflects the light of the Most High in her deeds.

3. **Serving in Marriage** – Submission is not oppression but divine alignment. A woman who serves her husband in love strengthens their union, making it a reflection of Yah's covenant with His people **(Ephesians 5:22-24)**.

4. **Serving in Ministry** – Ministry is not limited to the pulpit. A woman ministers through her hospitality, her encouragement, her wisdom, and her ability to intercede on behalf of others.

A woman who embraces servanthood is the backbone of her home, her marriage, and her community. She understands that servanthood is not a burden but a blessing. Through service, she strengthens her character, gains divine favor, and leaves a lasting legacy. As Yahusha served, so too must a righteous woman serve, knowing that in doing so, she fulfills her highest calling.

"The Strength to Serve"

I do not serve because I'm small,
But because I hear the Master's call.
Not chained by man, nor bound by fear—
I serve because His voice is near.

With hands prepared and spirit still,
I move in rhythm with His will.
Not for applause, nor worldly prize,
But for the favor in His eyes.

My service is not weakness worn,
It is where virtue is reborn.
To kneel is not to lose my place,
But to be covered by His grace.

I wash the feet, I bear the load,
I walk the long and narrow road.
For in this quiet, sacred task,
I wear a strength few ever ask.

I build the house, I calm the storm,
I tend the seed until it forms.
I rise at dawn, I stand at night,
A servant clothed in holy might.

I do not shrink, I do not fade,
I'm crafted from a rarer blade.
A warrior wrapped in warmth and light—
Who serves with joy, and fights with sight.

This is my crown, not made of gold—
But of obedience, firm and bold.
A helpmeet, servant, daughter, friend—
A vessel poured out 'til the end.

The Power of Inner Beauty

Growing up, I was obsessed with everything soft, feminine, and princess-like. I loved the sparkles, the elegance, the gowns—but what truly captivated me was the power each princess held. Their real "superpower" wasn't just magic—it was their **inner beauty**.

And just like in every story, when that inner beauty was absent—when hearts were dark, selfish, or cruel—those characters were cast as the wicked witch or the evil queen. That image stuck with me: a black heart versus a pure one. Because that's exactly how inner beauty works. It's the **color and condition of your heart**, your **character**, who you are when no one's watching.

This revelation started shaping my confidence in ways that makeup, clothes, or compliments never could. I had to learn how to embrace my awkward quirks, my quiet nature, and even my insecurities. I had to learn to show up authentically and with pure intentions.

What blew my mind was realizing that our inner beauty is deeply connected to our **spiritual countenance**. My private prayer life, my moments of worship and praise dancing before Yah, my reverence, my fear of Him—that was the transformation that shaped my glow. It became the light people were drawn to. It became my **spiritual lighthouse**, helping others find safety, peace, and a reminder of Yah's love.

Scriptures like Proverbs 31:30 and Sirach 18:19 remind us how essential self-examination and intentionality are. Inner beauty is the **integrity** between your desires and Yah's will. It's your secret life—the one no one sees—that spills out into your words, your posture, and your choices.

So yes, we can care for our outer beauty. But **inner beauty?** That's where the real royalty shines. It's what Yah sees. It's what the world feels. And it's what transforms not just you, but the lives of everyone connected to your light.

CHAPTER 8 THE ART OF INNER BEAUTY

"She shines from the inside out."

True beauty is not defined by outward adornment but by the radiance of a woman's spirit. A righteous woman shines from the inside out, reflecting the light of the Most High through her character, her wisdom, and her humility. While the world emphasizes external beauty, the Scriptures teach that inner beauty—rooted in faith, virtue, and a gentle spirit—is of far greater worth.

Inner beauty is the result of a woman's spiritual growth and connection with Yah. It is not something that can be bought, applied, or imitated—it is cultivated through righteousness, obedience, and a heart that seeks the Most High. As Proverbs 31:30 declares, *"Charm is deceitful, and beauty is vain, but a woman who fears Yah shall be praised."* A woman's reverence for the Most High transforms her from within, making her a vessel of peace, wisdom, and grace.

When a woman nurtures her spirit through prayer, Torah study, and righteous living, her countenance reflects that divine presence. This radiance is not fleeting but enduring, influencing those around her. Consider Moses when he descended from Mount Sinai—his face shone because he had been in the presence of Yah

(Exodus 34:29). Likewise, a woman who walks in the ways of the Most High carries an undeniable glow that is not dependent on physical features but on the spirit within her.

Biblical Women Who Exemplified Inner Beauty

- **Sarah (Genesis 18:12, 1 Peter 3:3-6)** – Sarah's beauty was not just in her appearance but in her submission, faith, and trust in Yah. She is honored in Scripture for her reverence and obedience, which made her a model for righteous women.

- **Hannah (1 Samuel 1:10-18)** – Though burdened with barrenness, Hannah's inner beauty shone through her unwavering faith and prayers. Her humility and devotion led Yah to bless her with a son, Samuel.

- **Esther (Esther 2:17, 4:16)** – Esther was chosen for her outward beauty, but it was her inner strength, courage, and wisdom that truly set her apart. Her selfless service to her people displayed a beauty deeper than physical appearance.

Outward Beauty vs. Inner Beauty

The world glorifies outer beauty, pushing women toward excessive adornment, vanity, and competition. However, Scripture warns against an overemphasis on outward appearance. *"Do not let your adornment be merely outward—arranging the hair, wearing gold, or putting on fine apparel—but let it be the hidden person of the heart, with the incorruptible beauty of a gentle and quiet spirit, which is very precious in the sight of Yah"* (1 Peter 3:3-4).

A woman who relies solely on external beauty will find it fading, but a woman who cultivates inner beauty will find her presence drawing others closer to Yah. Jezebel (2 Kings 9:30-37) adorned herself outwardly but lacked true righteousness, and her end was destruction. In contrast, a righteous woman's beauty endures beyond physical aging because it is rooted in her spirit. When a woman focuses on her spiritual growth, her entire being is transformed:

- **Her words carry wisdom and kindness (Proverbs 31:26).**
- **Her presence brings peace and comfort (Proverbs 14:1).**
- **Her actions reflect humility and grace (Philippians 2:3-4).**
- **Her relationships are strengthened by love and righteousness (Colossians 3:12-14).**

A woman who radiates inner beauty does not need validation from the world. She walks in confidence, knowing her worth comes from Yah.

Cultivating Inner Beauty in Daily Life

1. **Spiritual Nourishment** – A woman who prays, studies Torah, and seeks wisdom grows in beauty daily. Her spirit is refreshed, and she becomes a light to those around her.

2. **Humility and Gratitude** – True beauty is found in humility. A woman who serves others with a joyful heart reflects the beauty of the Most High.

3. **Speech and Conduct** – A righteous woman guards

her tongue, speaks life, and uplifts those around her **(Proverbs 15:4).**

4. **Patience and Gentleness** – The ability to remain patient, even in trials, reveals a beauty that is beyond external appearance **(James 1:4).**

5. **Righteous Living** – Walking in obedience to Yah's laws and being a virtuous example in the home and community enhances inner beauty.

She Shines from the Inside Out

A woman who embraces the art of inner beauty is a reflection of Yah's presence. Her radiance is not found in makeup, clothing, or jewelry, but in the light of her spirit. She shines not because of the world's standards but because she carries the essence of righteousness within her. As she grows in faith, wisdom, and virtue, her beauty becomes undeniable, influencing generations to come. Her light cannot be hidden, for she is the daughter of the Most High, and she shines from the inside out.

Selah Moment: The Mirror Within

Pause. Breathe. Listen.
You are more than what meets the eye. Your worth is not tied to curls, curves, skin, or style. Your Creator saw you, loved you, and called you good before you ever saw a mirror. Close your eyes for a moment and ask:
What does my soul wear today? *Is it clothed in comparison, or*

covered in compassion? Is it wrapped in fear, or robed in faith?

Let this truth settle deep:
Inner beauty is not a trend—it's a testimony. It is how you show up in a world that taught you to shrink. It is how you choose joy when bitterness is easier. It is how you love, even while healing.

Selah—pause and sit with that.

The Endurance Of The Will

*This wasn't about physical strength or how much I could lift or push through in my body. This was a different kind of endurance—one that tested my **will**. This was the place where **long-suffering** met reality.*

*Life brought with it twists and turns, unexpected moments designed to stretch my faith, deepen my steadfastness, and refine my spiritual maturity. I had to shift my perspective—I could no longer be caught off guard by every trial. Instead, I began to look for the test, not to be shaken, but to **pass it**.*

*I learned that life becomes easier when you live prepared. Of course, there will always be surprises, but they should only catch you off guard once. After that, you train. Every life event became a workout for my **inner growth**.*

I began to use my trials as a way to draw closer to Yah, just like Moses did. When his family spoke against him, he didn't retaliate—he ran to the Most High. When Yosef (Joseph) was thrown into the pit by his brothers, betrayed and misunderstood, he didn't try to vindicate himself—he cried out to Yah. These stories became blueprints.

*I learned to **commit my emotions to Yah**, to let Him sort what I should carry and what I should lay down. He started teaching me how to discern which battles were mine and which ones belonged to Him. He showed me how to balance my heart so it wouldn't faint, so I wouldn't spiral when things felt overwhelming or when people twisted the truth about me.*

*This kind of endurance taught me how to **stay in character**, to remain rooted in purpose and focused on what mattered most: **building**. Building my faith. Building my future. Building the spiritual legacy, He was calling me to carry. Because in the end, true endurance isn't about surviving—*
It's about growing stronger in the fire and trusting Yah through it all.

CHAPTER 9 THE ART OF ENDURANCE

"She built for this."

Life will test a woman in ways she never expected. There will be seasons of waiting, trials that feel unbearable, and moments when giving up seem like the only option. But a woman who walks with Yah understands—she is built for this. She carries within her the strength of those who came before, the resilience of the righteous women in Scripture who stood firm in the face of adversity. Endurance is not just about surviving; it's about pressing forward with faith, knowing that the Most High is refining her through every challenge.

The Word is full of women who endured hardship but remained steadfast in their faith. Their stories are not just historical accounts but living testimonies of what it means to trust in Yah even when the path is unclear.

- **Hagar (Genesis 16; 21:14-21)** – A woman cast out into the wilderness with her child, Hagar faced uncertainty and fear. But Yah heard her cries and provided for her and Ishmael, showing that even when all seems lost, He makes a way.

- **Ruth (Ruth 1-4)** – A widow in a foreign land, Ruth could have turned back to her old life. Instead, she chose faithfulness, endurance, and hard work, leading her to a new beginning and a place in the lineage of Yahusha.

- **Hannah (1 Samuel 1:1-20)** – In the face of barrenness and mockery, Hannah did not waver. She poured her soul out in prayer, enduring years of heartache until Yah answered her with the birth of Samuel.

- **The Woman with the Issue of Blood (Mark 5:25-34)** – Twelve years of suffering did not stop her from reaching out in faith. One touch of Yahusha's garment changed everything, proving that endurance leads to deliverance.

Endurance is not passive—it's an active stance in the spirit. It means standing firm when trials press in, keeping faith when answers seem distant, and continuing forward when the weight of life feels overwhelming. Endurance is:

- **Trusting Yah's Timing** – Like Sarah, who waited decades for the promised child, we must trust that what Yah has spoken will come to pass in His perfect time.

- **Pushing Forward Despite Fear** – Like Esther, who risked her life to save her people, endurance means walking in faith even when fear is present.

- **Remaining Faithful in Hardship** – Like the widow of Zarephath, who had only enough flour and oil for one last meal, endurance means believing that Yah will provide even when resources are scarce.

If you find yourself in a season of struggle, know that you are not alone. The Most High sees you, hears your prayers, and is strengthening you through this process. Trials are not designed to break you but to build you, molding you into a vessel of wisdom, patience, and faith. As Romans 5:3-4 reminds us: *"We glory in tribulations also: knowing that tribulation worketh patience; and patience, experience; and experience, hope."*

Here are some ways to endure with strength and grace:

1. **Keep Your Eyes on Yah** – When trials come, shift your focus from the problem to the One who holds the

solution. Worship, pray, and meditate on His Word daily.

2. **Remember Who You Are** – You are a daughter of the Most High, built with the endurance of the women who came before you. Their strength is in your spiritual DNA.

3. **Surround Yourself with Faithful Women** – Endurance is strengthened in community. Seek out righteous sisters who will uplift you, pray with you, and remind you of Yah's promises.

4. **Rest When needed, but Don't Quit** – Even Yahusha took moments of rest. Endurance is not about never pausing —it's about knowing when to refresh so you can keep going.

5. **Speak Life Over Yourself** – Declare the promises of Yah. Speak strength over your situation. Remind yourself that you are built for this.

She's Built for This

A woman who endures is a woman who overcomes. She does not break under pressure—she bends, adjusts, and rises stronger. Her trials do not define her; her faith does. Through every storm, she remembers: she is built for this. Yah has equipped her with everything she needs to endure, and on the other side of her perseverance is victory. Keep going, daughter of Zion—your endurance is not in vain.

Selah Moment: The Strength to Keep Going

Pause. Breathe. Be still.
You have walked through fire and didn't burn. You've carried things that would've crushed others. Yet here you are—still becoming.

Endurance is not just surviving—it is trusting while tired, believing while breaking, worshiping while waiting. You don't have to feel strong to be strong.
Even your quiet tears are laced with glory. Even your stillness is warfare when you stay rooted in Him.

Selah—breathe in the truth of that.

You are not running alone. The Most High walks with you. He strengthens your feet like a deer—to climb the high places without falling.
Where in your life do you feel weary right now?
What would it look like to lean instead of push?
Write a short prayer of surrender, asking Yah to exchange your exhaustion for endurance.

A Legacy Worth Living

I pray to leave behind a powerful, empowering legacy for my children —one that speaks long after I'm gone. Growing up, my maternal grandmother quietly handed me a legacy of strength through her prayer life. She didn't have to say much—I watched her live it.

Every morning, she rose early to read and study the Word. I saw how seriously she honored Shabbat—how she gave that day entirely to Elohim and to the people she served. She spent the whole day pouring into her assembly and caring for the needs of even the smallest members of her community. Her pursuit of truth was physical, tangible—and her inner beauty radiated through her actions more than her words.

That legacy didn't stop with her. I saw it carried in her children. My mother's strength. My aunts' sisterhood, love, and unwavering support. I was surrounded by virtuous women who weren't just surviving life—they were intentionally building a world for their children to thrive in.

And on the other side, my paternal grandmother left a different kind of legacy—one I witnessed in the faces of the many lives she touched. I saw it in the stories, the tears, the joy and laughter shared at her funeral. Her impact stretched beyond her household; her life spoke volumes through the people she served and loved.

*That's when it hit me: **Time is the greatest equalizer.***

*Everything we do—from the way we serve, to the way we use our gifts, to the divine appointments we keep—all of it births our legacy. Every encounter, every sacrifice, every creation, and every act of obedience to Yah's purpose becomes part of the story our lives are writing. **Legacy is the movie your life creates.***
And when it plays back, make sure it's a story that inspires generations...
A story that gives Yah all the glory

CHAPTER 10 THE ART OF LEGACY

"She leavin' her mark."

A righteous woman doesn't just live for today—she walks with eternity in mind. Everything she does, every seed she plants, every lesson she teaches, every act of love and faith she pours out is building something beyond herself. She understands that her life is not just about her own journey but about the generations coming after her. Legacy isn't just about what you leave behind—it's about who you build up along the way.

Legacy isn't just about material wealth or accomplishments; it's about the spiritual, moral, and cultural foundation you lay for those who follow. It's the wisdom you pass down, the example you set, the faith you cultivate in your home and community. A righteous woman's legacy is felt long after she's gone because she has sown seeds that continue to bear fruit.

Proverbs 31:28 says, *"Her children arise up, and call her blessed; her husband also, and he praises her."* **That is legacy—living in such a way that your impact outlasts your years, shaping the lives of those who come after you.

Throughout Scripture, we see women who left powerful legacies through their faith, wisdom, and righteous actions:

- **Sarah (Genesis 17:15-21)** – The mother of nations, her faith in Yah's promise established an everlasting covenant.

- **Miriam (Exodus 15:20-21)** – A prophetess and leader, she played a key role in guiding and inspiring Israel.

- **Deborah (Judges 4-5)** – A judge and warrior, she led Israel with wisdom and courage, leaving behind a legacy of strength and leadership.

- **Lois and Eunice (2 Timothy 1:5)** – The grandmother and mother of Timothy, they passed down sincere faith, ensuring that righteousness continued through their lineage.

Leaving a righteous legacy requires intention, consistency, and faith. Here are ways to ensure that what you build lasts beyond your lifetime:

1. **Live by Example** – The most powerful lessons aren't just taught; they're lived. Let your children, community, and spiritual family see faith in action through your daily walk.

2. **Teach and Impart Wisdom** – Pass down the knowledge of Torah, the lessons of life, and the wisdom of righteousness. Speak truth into the next generation.

3. **Build Strong Relationships** – Legacy is not built in isolation. Pour into those around you, especially younger women who will carry the torch forward.

4. **Stay Rooted in Faith** – A legacy of righteousness begins with unwavering devotion to Yah. Your consistency in prayer, obedience, and worship lays a foundation for those after you.

5. **Leave Something Tangible** – Whether it's written words, traditions, a ministry, or a way of life, create something that can be passed down and continued.

There will be times when you wonder if your efforts matter, if the seeds you're planting will grow. But remember, Yah is the one who gives the increase. Your obedience, faith, and love will not return void. Even when you don't see the results immediately, trust that you are shaping something bigger than yourself.

Ecclesiastes 3:14 says, *"I know that, whatsoever God doeth, it shall be forever: nothing can be put to it, nor anything taken from it: and God doeth it, that men should fear before him."* What Yah builds through you will last.

She Leavin' Her Mark

A righteous woman doesn't just exist—she *builds.* She pours into the next generation, she nurtures faith, she strengthens her home, and she creates something that endures. Whether it's in her children, her community, her wisdom, or her example, her presence is felt even when she's no longer here. She is a planter of seeds, a bearer of light, and a keeper of truth.

Sis, you are not just living for today. You are writing history, shaping the future, and building something eternal. Keep pressing forward, keep sowing, keep shining—because you are leaving your mark.

Selah Moment: Pause. Breathe. Reflect.

Legacy is not just what you leave behind—it's what you plant while you're here. It's the fruit of your choices, the sound of your wisdom, the echo of your obedience. You are someone's answered prayer. You carry the strength of generations who prayed, wept, and warred in silence. You are the link between what was and what will be.

Selah—breathe in the weight and wonder of that.

Your legacy is shaped not just by loud moments, but by quiet faithfulness,
by the way you love, by the truth you live when no one is looking. You are not just living for now. You are building for forever. What seeds are you sowing that will bless those who come after you? What do you want your children—or your community—to say you stood for? Write a declaration of the legacy you are committed to building with Yah's help.

Manifestation—The Power To Align

Oh boy— **"manifestation"** has become a spooky word in today's world. With witches and warlocks parading boldly, and mental health under spiritual attack masked as new-age enlightenment, the word often carries the wrong weight. But let's ask an honest question: Why do we believe that only the wicked can manifest things in this world—and not the righteous?

The truth is, the enemy is the greatest imitator. But **Yahuah is the only Creator.** And He made us in His image—especially women—as **co-creators.** There is power in what we build, shape, nurture, and speak into existence.

Yah began to teach me that in any building process, there's always an **overseer**—someone who sees the blueprint, speaks it aloud, and sets the work in motion. That's who we are. The words we declare shift the very atmosphere. Our imaginations push the limits of our belief, and that belief, when in alignment with Yah's will, births tangible results.

I used to think my constant daydreaming was a bad habit. Teachers always told me, "Stop daydreaming! Get focused!" But then Yah showed me—my imagination wasn't the problem. It was meant to be a **meeting place** for Him—a space where He could speak, reveal, and even train me for spiritual warfare. I had to learn that what I imagined—good or bad—was a seed. And whatever seed I watered most would become my reality.

I started realizing that this physical world? It's a shadow. The **unseen** is what governs the **seen.** That flipped everything for me. I had to start steering my thoughts like a ship headed toward righteousness. No more letting my imagination wander into fear, doubt, or false identities. I had to **sanctify** that space and invite Yah to dwell in it.

Manifestation is not just about seeing your dreams come to life. It's a **confirmation** that your prayers are being answered. It's like Daniel— when he prayed, the answer was released in the spirit, but it took time to show up in the physical. He had to stay focused on Yah's sovereignty and resist the temptation to doubt. If he had shifted into fear, the spiritual battle would've tipped—and nothing would've manifested at all.

That's what happens to us. Sometimes our prayers go unanswered because we cancel them with our unbelief. We have to stand firm and believe that **Yahuah is faithful to perform His word**—if we've done our part.

Manifestation, then, is about **confidence**. It's about walking boldly, speaking with clarity, and thinking righteously. It's the result of being in right standing with Yah, knowing that Deuteronomy 28 blessings are tracking you down—not the curses.

When you live blamelessly before the Most High, creation responds—not to your ego, but to your alignment.

CHAPTER 11 THE ART OF MANIFESTATION

"She spoke it, now she walkin' in it."

Manifestation isn't just about speaking things into existence—it's about aligning your faith, your actions, and your mindset with what Yah has already placed in you. A righteous woman doesn't just dream; she moves. She co-creates with The Father, taking the vision given to her and bringing it into reality with wisdom, faith, and work. She understands that the power to build, nurture, and expand is in her hands when she partners with Yah.

Words carry power. Proverbs 18:21 reminds us that *"Death and life are in the power of the tongue."* What you speak over yourself, your household, and your destiny shapes the atmosphere around you. But words without action are empty. Manifestation requires movement.

A woman of Yah does not just hope—she prepares. She does not just wish—she works. She does not just pray—she obeys. She walks as if the promise is already hers, making room for the blessings she knows are on the way. Faith without works is dead **(James 2:26)**, so if she believes Yah will provide, she moves like it's already done.

A woman's spiritual growth shows up in tangible ways. **Galatians 5:22-23** lays out the *fruits of the Spirit—**Love, Joy, Peace, Patience, Kindness, Goodness, Faithfulness, Gentleness, and Self-Control**.* These are the markers of a life aligned with Yah's will.

- **Love** – She moves in love, not just in words but in action, building up her family and community.

- **Joy** – Her spirit is not easily shaken because her joy comes from Yah, not circumstances.

- **Peace** – She carries an atmosphere of shalom, bringing calmness even in chaos.

- **Patience** – She understands timing and does not rush what Yah is perfecting.

- **Kindness & Goodness** – She extends grace and goodness to others, sowing seeds that will multiply.

- **Faithfulness** – She remains steadfast in her purpose and committed to Yah's plan.

- **Gentleness & Self-Control** – She walks with wisdom, knowing that discipline and discernment sustain what she builds.

When a woman cultivates these fruits, the evidence of Yah's work in her life becomes undeniable. She is manifesting His presence in every step she takes.

Favor isn't about luck—it's about positioning. When a woman aligns herself with Yah's will, she moves in favor because she is walking in obedience. Proverbs 3:5-6 says, *"Trust in the Lord with all thine heart; and lean not unto thine own understanding. In all thy ways acknowledge Him, and He shall direct thy paths."*

Favor comes when a woman:

- Seeks Yah first in all things **(Matthew 6:33)**

- Moves with wisdom and understanding (Proverbs 4:7)

- Walks in righteousness, knowing obedience brings blessings **(Deuteronomy 28:1-2)**

- Guards her mind and tongue, speaking life and not destruction

- Serves and builds, knowing that what she sows, she will reap

When she moves in this way, doors open, opportunities arise, and people are drawn to the light she carries. She doesn't chase—she attracts, because she is in divine flow with Yah's purpose for her life.

A woman operates in *Binah*—the gift of understanding. She takes the vision and adds the details. She brings form to what was once just an idea. In a home, a community, or a nation, it is often the woman who takes the seed and nurtures it into something great.

- A husband provides the vision; she organizes, structures, and makes it flourish.
- A community needs a foundation; she brings the culture, wisdom, and sustenance.
- A child is born; she nurtures and educates them, shaping the next generation.

The Most High gives vision, and the woman brings it to life with the depth of her understanding. She is a bridge between thought and reality, making things happen through faith, wisdom, and diligence.

She Walks in It

Manifestation is about more than getting what you want—it's about stepping fully into the purpose Yah has for you. It's about being a vessel for His will, allowing His favor to flow through you, and using your God-given wisdom to bring greatness into reality.

A righteous woman speaks it, believes it, moves in it, and watches it unfold. She partners with Yah, knowing that with Him, all things are possible. She doesn't just wait for her blessings—she makes room for them. She doesn't just hope for change—she *is* the change. She spoke it. Now she's walkin' in it.

Selah Moment: Becoming What You Speak

Pause. Breathe. Be still.
Before you manifest anything outwardly—ask yourself:
Has my heart aligned with heaven?

True manifestation begins in the secret place. Not with chasing, not with striving,
but with agreeing with what the Most High has already spoken over your life. What are you calling forth? And does it reflect His will—or your wants?

Selah—rest here for a moment.

What vision has Yah placed in your heart that you've been afraid to fully walk into? What do you need to release—or become—to carry it with honor?

short affirmation:
"I am becoming the woman who can carry what I prayed for."

"When Heaven Meets Earth"

It starts not with hands, but with heart,
A whisper where heaven and soul both start.
Not wishing wild, nor chasing wind,
But aligning deep with what's within.

The Word I speak must first be sown,
In soil of trust, in faith alone.
Not forced by flesh or fleeting trend,
But led by Ruach, without end.

I close my eyes, yet see it clear—
The vision placed by YAH draws near.
Not mine to mold with vain intent,
But shaped through prayer and covenant.

Each thought a seed, each step a vow,
I plant with praise, I water now.
With patience robed in sacred fire,
I move in rhythm, not in tire.

For manifestation is not haste—
It's timing wrapped in holy grace.
It is the fruit of hands made clean,
Of walking out what's yet unseen.

I don't just speak—I become the word,
A living promise, shaped and stirred.
The kingdom lives in what I birth—
When faith and works collide on earth.

The Beauty of Becoming Perfect

*Being perfect doesn't look anything like the world's impossible standards. The world taught me that perfection meant never making a mistake, never wrestling with my flaws, my triggers, or my traumas. It taught me to perform—to put on a mask and act like I had it all together, even when I was silently screaming for mentorship... praying not to be thrust into leadership too soon. And yet, while I was breaking on the inside, the Most High was building me. He was shaping me into **His** perfection.*

*Scripture reminds us: "Man looks at the outward appearance, but YAH looks at the heart." – **1 Samuel 16:7***

*In Hebraic understanding, true perfection is called **Tamim**—a word that means whole, complete, sound, and mature. It's not about flawlessness. It's about living in integrity and being fully aligned with the will of the Creator. And how do we live this out? Through our **Halakah**.*

*Halakah (also spelled Halakhah) comes from the Hebrew root **halak** (הָלַךְ), meaning "to walk" or "to go." It's more than religious law. It is a living path—a daily journey that reflects how we walk with YAH in obedience, humility, devotion, and character.*

Halakah is not just about what we do—it's about who we are becoming. It's how we treat others, how we carry truth, how we respond to correction, and how we keep walking, even when the road is hard. It is your spiritual journey—your step-by-step refining process as you walk before YAH, becoming more like Him with every test, every gate, and every season.

*"Walk before Me and be thou perfect (Tamim)." – **Genesis 17:1***

*To walk in Halakah is to say: "**I choose to grow. I choose to yield. I choose to walk the ancient path that leads to life.**"*

I'm still very young. I haven't arrived—but I am walking. As I stay *focused, practice the Twelve Gates, and remain faithful, I will become fully developed. My **integrity** will increase. My **alignment** with TMH will deepen.*

*So, I ask that you continue to pray—for your Halakah and for mine. May we all mature and persevere in these trying times... that we may be counted as **Tamim**—perfect, whole, and pleasing in our generation.*

CHAPTER 12 THE ART OF BECOMING PERFECT OR TAMIM

"She handles hers."

Being a woman of Yah means handling your responsibilities, staying on top of things, and moving with purpose. A functional woman is dependable, self-sufficient, and does what needs to be done without excuses. But handling yours isn't just about getting through day-to-day—it's about growing into the fullness of who Yah created you to be. In Hebrew, the word *tamim* (תָּמִים) Is often translated as "perfect," but it doesn't mean without flaw. It means whole, complete, mature in faith. A righteous woman isn't chasing flawlessness; she's walking in wholeness.

The root of tamim (תָּם) means "complete, whole, sound, or finished." In the Hebraic mindset, perfection isn't about never making mistakes; it's about being fully developed, walking with integrity, and living in alignment with Yah's will. This concept is woven throughout Scripture:

- *Genesis 6:9 – "Noah was a righteous man, perfect (tamim) in his generations. Noah walked with Elohim."*

- *Psalm 119:1 – "Blessed are the undefiled (tamim) in the way, who walk in the law of the Lord."*

These verses show that tamim is not about flawlessness, but about being spiritually whole, mature, and unwavering in faith.

Deuteronomy 18:13 says, *"Thou shalt be perfect (tamim) with the Lord thy God."* This isn't a call to be without mistakes; it's a call to be fully committed to Yah, lacking nothing in your faith and devotion. The concept of *tamim* is about spiritual integrity. It means living in a way that reflects Yah's truth in every aspect of your life—your mind, your heart, your actions, and your relationships.

- **Wholeness in Faith** – Walking in trust, knowing that Yah's plan is greater than you're understanding.

- **Wholeness in Character** – Being the same woman in private that you are in public, with honesty and righteousness.

- **Wholeness in Purpose** – Operating in alignment with Yah's will, using your gifts to serve and build.

Wholeness isn't an overnight transformation—it's a process, a journey of refining and shaping. Yah works in seasons, and every trial, lesson, and experience is designed to grow you into the woman He intends you to be.

1. **Self-Reflection:** You can't grow if you don't check yourself. What areas of your life need work? What habits are holding you back?

2. **Surrender:** Trust that Yah is the master builder. When He removes something from your life, it's because He's making space for better.

3. **Discipline:** Spiritual maturity requires consistency. Prayer, study, fasting—these aren't just rituals; they're tools for becoming whole.

4. **Resilience:** Every righteous woman has faced challenges, but it's her endurance that makes her *tamim*. When hardships come, she doesn't break—she grows.

The ultimate example of *tamim* is Yahusha . He walked in complete obedience, full of grace, wisdom, and power. He was whole, lacking nothing, fully surrendered to the Father's will.

To be *tamim* is to strive to be like Him:

- **Moving with Wisdom** – Speaking with discernment, knowing when to act and when to be still.

- **Serving with Love** – Putting others before yourself, not for recognition, but because it's the right thing to do.

- **Walking in Strength** – Facing trials with faith, knowing that suffering produces endurance (Romans 5:3-4).

A woman on the path to *tamim* understands that mistakes happen, but she doesn't dwell in them. She learns, she adjusts, and she keeps moving forward. She doesn't let guilt or shame keep her stuck—she repents, she resets, and she rises.

She handles hers. She walks in purpose. She becomes whole, lacking nothing, because she is fully grounded in Yah.

Tamim isn't about being flawless—it's about being faithful.

Beloved daughter of Zion, you've made it to the end—but really, this is just the beginning. You've been invited into something far greater than checking off spiritual boxes or simply surviving each day. You've been called to *become*—to rise into the woman Yah created you to be: whole, complete, and mature in your faith.

This journey isn't about looking perfect. It's about walking with purpose. It's about spiritual integrity, inner alignment, and unwavering devotion to the Most High. To be a woman of Yah is to live responsibly, love deeply, speak wisely, and grow continually.

You handle yours—not out of pride, but out of obedience.
Because you understand that your life is not your own. You were chosen. Set apart. Called for such a time as this.

But now what? Now that you've received these truths—what will you *do* with them?

This is your moment to choose the narrow path.
To walk in **Halakah**—a life aligned with the ancient way.
To build, heal, serve, nurture, and *become*.

So here is your ***call to action:***

- **Self-reflect:** Regularly examine your heart, your habits, your fruit.
- **Stay teachable:** Seek counsel, mentorship, and community with other righteous women.
- **Cultivate discipline:** Carve out sacred time for prayer, fasting, study, and stillness.
- **Serve with love:** Use your gifts. Build others. Be a blessing.
- **Endure with strength:** When storms come—and they will—lean on Yah. Let your faith be unshakable.
- **Move with intention:** Stop waiting for a "better season." This is the season. Start walking now.

This walk isn't about perfection in the world's eyes.
It's about becoming **Tamim**—a woman fully grounded, fully whole, and fully faithful. Let your life be the evidence. Let your wholeness be your worship.
Let every step you take echo,
"I am becoming the woman Yah destined me to be."

Now rise, daughter.
And *walk.*
Because *He who began a good work in you will be faithful to complete it* **(Philippians 1:6).**

MORAH CHAYILYAH SEGULAH

You were born to be Tamim.

ABOUT THE AUTHOR

Morah Chayilyah Segulah

Morah Chayilyah Segulah is a Holistic Doula, Teacher, Life Coach, and Healer with over a decade of experience. She is passionate about guiding women to grow in maturity, walk in purpose, and stand as pillars in their homes and communities. Her work blends ancient truths with practical tools, helping  women heal, grow, and walk boldly in their divine assignments. Known for her deeply spiritual and culturally rooted approach, She inspires transformation from the inside out.

www.ingramcontent.com/pod-product-compliance
Lightning Source LLC
Chambersburg PA
CBHW071533120626
46550CB00006B/2436

* 9 7 9 8 8 9 7 7 8 4 6 3 9 *